"Cathy takes biblical stories of encounters with Jesus that we're all familiar with. Then she dips the paintbrush of imagination and revelation and vividly 'colorizes' those stories—and suddenly—the encounter with Jesus was not just for another person, not for another time or place in dusty history, but a deeply moving encounter for each of us, right here, right now at this very moment. Her probing reflections with each chapter will bring fresh insights and deep healing. This is a powerful and important book...for all of us!"

—*Nancy Stafford, Actress (Co-star TV's "Matlock"), Speaker and Author of* The Wonder of His Love: A Journey into the Heart of God, *and* Beauty by the Book: Seeing Yourself as God Sees You

"As a follower of Christ for more than half a century, I have read the stories of Christ, listened to them, and seen them portrayed. In the pages of this book, I lived and felt them. Thanks, Cathy, for taking me on the rich adventure!"

—*Larry W. Poland, Ph.D., Chairman and CEO, Mastermedia International*

"A sanctified imagination is a gift from God. Cathy Heiliger's expression of this gift is exceptional. In *Encounters of the Heart,* her ability to connect imaginative back-stories with the biblical narrative of her character's lives will cause the reader to feel like she is right there, on the scene, as Jesus did His wonderful works.

As I read this book, I felt my Savior's touch afresh in my own life and circumstances. Cathy's portrayal of the stories of Christ's loving compassion during His earthly ministry brings that same compassion squarely into the 21st century and will convince us all that our Lord still cares enough to meet us where we are and lavish His love on us, meeting whatever needs we might have. If you need a personal touch from Jesus in your life, this is the book for you."

—*Steve McVey, author,* Grace Walk

"Ever wonder what's behind the scene in a biblical story? This book opens the door to imagination and insight. Cathy does a wonderful job of uncovering what the authors and characters of these biblical stories must have been thinking and feeling. This book really gives a human picture to biblical truth. This is a MUST read!"
—*Randy and Cathy Alward, President, CEO Maranatha Music*

"As one captured by the power of story, I see *Encounters of the Heart,* as a rich resource to support the Christian pulpit by adding poetry and prose to the biblical narrative. This book is full of wisdom and adds dramatic language to good exegetical work to support teachers, pastors, songwriters, and speakers in their vocational pursuit to see transformed lives."
—*Bill Twyman, The Vineyard Churches National Board of Directors, President/Founder of the Trinity Learning Community Graduate School of Ministry, Senior Pastor of Inland Vineyard Christian Fellowship, Corona, CA*

"This is one of the most exciting books we have read in a long time. While it is theologically sound, it is also experientially riveting—we laughed and cried as the Holy Spirit touched us through these anointed stories of Jesus written for the 21st century."
—*Pastors Tony and Janet Alward, Word of Life Ministries*

ENCOUNTERS
→ OF THE ←
Heart

ENCOUNTERS
→ OF THE ←

Heart

There's
More to
the Story
Than
Meets the
Eye

CATHY HEILIGER

Evergreen
PRESS

Mobile, AL

ISBN 978-1-58169-247-1
For Worldwide Distribution
Printed in the U.S.A.

Evergreen Press
P.O. Box 191540 • Mobile, AL 36619

Table of Contents

ACKNOWLEDGMENTS

To my husband and best friend, Bruce: I love you for being the closest touch-point of the Father's affection to me for 32 years. The hoisting of this sail on "The Ship" is because of your encouragement and foresight. Thank you, honey, for helping me catch the wind of the Spirit!

To my sons and daughters, Nicole, Joshua, Eric and Stevie: My encounters with you have, and will continue, to teach me more than I could ever have hoped for. I love and thank you with all my heart.

To my grand-girls Gracie, Ava, and Shaelyn Rose: Thank you for reminding me how to stay "little."

Mom: No one on earth has had a greater influence on my life. I am beyond blessed to have been so nurtured, tutored, and befriended.

Bob: Thank you for being such a willing and helpful stepfa-ther/reader/editor, and rocket-scientist!

To my sibs, Rob, Evelyn, Steve, Melissa, and Mary: Thanks for your encouragement and celebration. Hop on the plane and let's take this ride together!

To all the friends who have loved me to life: Brian and Tiffany Woodward, Marge Schultz, Ron and Eleanor Barley, Bill and Pam Twyman, Nancy Stafford, Noma DuCharme, Carolyn Bible, Pam Brown, Dr. Dennis and Pat Conneen, MaryBeth Stafford, Doctors Len and Patty Cerny, Craig and Tamra Holland, Shawn and "V" Johnson, Dan and Michelle

Linscott, Carla Malden, Bill and Betsy Jackson, Nancy Chance (whose therapeutic massage kept my body intact), Ed McGlasson, Dr. Larry Poland, Mike and Marla Maynard, Teri Awad, Mindy Ogden, Carol Pierce, Beth Rowland, Julie Tegeler, Tom and GiGi Hull, John and Paula Sandford, Leanne Payne, and C.S. Lewis: Thank you for your friendship, prayers, encouragements, mentorings, readings, feedback, and dinners out!

And finally to Kris and Lori Huff, and Colin and Melanie Cumbee, whose Big Bear home provided shelter and solace to "lead me beside still waters, restoring my soul." Your place has helped me find my place.

INTRODUCTION

I've always hungered to read about biblical characters in a dimensional way that helped me relate to them as real-time people with bad breath and dysfunctional thinking. I've yearned to climb into the skins of those whom Jesus encountered. I've wanted to come to know them through their hypothetical "back-stories," and experience his power in rewriting their "future-stories" and mine!

Encounters of the Heart intends to bring fact and fiction together to fill in the blanks, calling biblical personalities to life for the 21st century. As you read these first-person short stories, I would encourage you to sink into the soul of the character about whom you're reading. You just might find their heart is very much like your own.

I have purposed to follow the biblical storyline in all its power while concentrating on the emotional aspect of humans in contact with Jesus as he made himself known as Messiah. I have no intention of adding or subtracting from the Gospel texts, nor of rewriting any of the Scripture. Indeed, I am keenly aware of the biblical warnings against it. I have, however, relied upon scholars who have broken down the original Greek texts into English and have utilized more specific Greek-oriented terminology in Jesus' dialogue than what may be recorded in modern translations.

In this work, I've also begun experiencing more fully the power of a rightly used imagination. My hope is that, by reverently "colorizing" the scriptural encounters of Christ with the scents, textures, and dynamics of conceivable human life in biblical times, the reader will experience a greater personal knowledge of the three-dimensional risen Christ, and the "Spirit of the Word" that resides in all the Scriptures.

Cathy Heiliger
Riverside, California, July 2007

Chapter One

A WOMAN AND HER ISSUE

Luke 8:40-48

I sat on the rough ground, leaning against a tree that morning, attempting to find a precious hour of sleep that would carry me away from the reality of my wretched life. My breathing had become more labored than ever before. I wondered if it was because the air was so hot and humid that day. The sticky weather added an even further burden to my already exhausted frame.

A fly landed in my ear, and the buzzing of it irritated me. Laying my head back against the tree, I scanned the rolling hills that were the color of yellow onions surrounding the Sea of Galilee. I used to hate living here. The hot wind had made my skin dry and leathery, and my mouth always tasted of sand. But in the last twelve years, the desert and I had become close friends. We understood each other's desolation. We comprehended similar places of loneliness and thirst. We both longed for refreshment, but neither of us had found an oasis.

That morning, however, my eyes looked beyond the familiar landscape. A clamor arose from the people near the water's edge. Women far from the shore were running toward a boat with three sails that was just docking. Many people seemed to be raising their hands in some kind of odd celebration. Fathers galloped toward the water with little children on their backs, and old people hobbled along on arthritic knees— everyone clamoring for whatever it was that was drawing their attention.

"A load of carp," I said to myself.

I sank down onto my right side, the only position I could find to stay comfortable. My lower back felt as inflamed as a rack of lamb on a spit. My nose inadvertently passed over my armpit and made me gag. I just couldn't stomach the stench.

Rolling over, my face in the sand, I started to scream, "Let me into heaven! I would rather die than live like this!"

But as soon as my lungs pressed against my thin ribs, that warm, dreaded gush poured out from underneath me, and I had to hobble again behind the tree so no one would see. The rags were so old, so thin that they hardly helped anymore. I had nothing left. What was I going to do?

I fell down in a bundle, hunched over, too tired to cry, and yet, this time, I did.

"How long, O Lord? How long before you let me die?"

The crowd from the shore began sprinting past me into town, their voices vibrating with jubilation. Although I felt too despondent to care, I glanced up to see what was happening. A younger man in the center of the throng was walking with Jairus, who I knew was the overseer of our synagogue here in Capernaum. Jairus looked like he had just gotten out of bed. *Strange for a man of such personal tidiness,* I thought. *Why was he wearing only a tunic?*

One of my former neighbors swept by me and spat on the

ground, dismissing me completely. Although I wasn't a leper, I was treated like one. "Unclean" had become my middle name.

I crouched farther away, moving as fast as I could to get away from the throng, but for some reason I was drawn to look again. Suddenly I was captivated by the most dazzling sight I'd ever beheld—two compassionate, magnificent eyes that were looking straight at me. They were the eyes of the man walking briskly with Jairus. I was afraid to hold his gaze, but I couldn't help myself. For a moment I was paralyzed. I don't think I moved until someone shouted, "Jesus! Jesus of Nazareth! The Messiah is come!"

Indescribably, with the very mention of that name, something inside me leapt. Jesus! I had heard of this man! *He heals the sick. Would he . . . ? Do I dare? Oh, my God, my Elohim.*

Unconsciously, I started moving toward him until I remembered the shame of my robe. I cursed at the red on the back of my cloak, reaching for the only thing that made a difference—the water I always carried with me in a flask. I pulled my robe around and poured the water over the stain until it washed away into the sand. Oh that someone would do just that for my heart! But physicians cannot heal broken hearts. And often, they cannot heal broken bodies.

I shuddered, remembering their prescriptions. They made me drink wine boiled with nine Persian onions and then proclaimed: "Arise from thy flux." But that failed. Next, one of them said: "Set her in a place where two ways meet, and let her hold a cup of wine in her hand. Have somebody come behind her to frighten her and say, 'Arise from thy flux.'" They did frighten me, but the only result was their wine-stained clothing! The most humiliating was their instruction to dig seven trenches and burn some cuttings from vines in them. They put a cup of wine in my hand and led me to squat down over each trench. They proclaimed once again: "Arise from thy flux," but my legs buckled under me from the cramping. When I fell, the doctors didn't even pick me up. They couldn't touch me. I was ritually unclean.[1]

It had been twelve years since I had entered the synagogue. My friends used to call me "David's sister," because I led the dance worshippers in procession to the Temple. My "issue," however, prohibited me from even the most casual touch, because if someone touched me, they were unclean for seven days. For too many years, no one's hand had caressed my face; no friend had knelt down to pray for my heart; no husband had...

Was it any wonder I felt so despairing?

The cramping was so bad I was hunched over most of the time. In some ways, maybe that was a benefit. No one could see who I was. I had come to believe maybe it was easier to be ill than to be well. No one expected anything from me. I had certainly come to not expect anything from myself.

But those eyes had seen me, really seen me. I don't know how, but I felt like Jesus knew me. I had to hear him. Something was compelling me to draw closer to him. Despite my worry about the odor, I knew I had to reach him. I swung a burlap scarf around my head, and although the day was hot, my head began to cool just at the thought that I might be close, once more, to those eyes.

As I put one foot in front of the other, a strange strength began to propel me. I looked at the massive crowd encircling the young teacher, and being as thin as I was, I thought: *Maybe I can maneuver in through these people just enough to touch the hem of his robe. If I could only touch, for just an instant, something of his...for some reason I know I will be well.*

I plunged into the jostling crowd, but I was pushed away. Someone kicked me, and I fell. A man, smelling like stale wine, stepped on my hand. A woman with fat arms shoved me to the side. The dust began choking me, and my eyes had trouble focusing.

Is this worth it? I wondered as someone stomped on my foot. *Is moving toward him worth the cost?* But I remembered the compassion, the—dare I say—friendship in his eyes? I got up and said to myself, "I must have whatever he gives. No one else has dared to look at me like that since I became ill."

The frenzy of the crowd was rising, and people were fainting from bodies crushing each other trying to get to this teacher. Some fishermen were surrounding him, locking arms, yelling to each other to stay connected, as though they were a life preserver around a drowning man in the sea. Panic, fear, and anger flashed in people's eyes. Waves of pressed flesh began squeezing, pushing, and battering Jesus so violently that he had to climb on someone's shoulders to be able to catch his breath.

It was a frightening pit of people to be in! I came close to leaving, terrified of the stampede. But then I saw my chance. His robe was a yard in front of me! I reached for it, strained for it, but a group of angry men pushed him away. I couldn't breathe and started to choke. I stood up for air, terrified that someone would notice me and took another deep breath. *One more try.*

I elbowed my way next to one of his fish-smelling friends, a large brute with bad breath and a rowdy laugh. He had to strong-arm a man away from tearing the young teacher's robe, and as he did, I saw a little opening that I might be able my way through.

If I can just touch his garment, I will be well!

I closed my eyes, pushed, and dove through the hole in the mass of people. I stretched with all my might toward the blue tassel on his robe. Suddenly something brushed me like the feathers of a bird's wing, and for some reason, I remembered the ancient Psalm: "Under his wings you will find refuge."

Oh! Oh, my God!

Suddenly, I felt like warm honey had been poured into my veins. It was like I was being bathed in the sparkles I saw on the sea at dawn. I almost couldn't let go of the robe! Immediately, my hemorrhaging...stopped! My heart began to beat stronger. I felt color flowing into my cheeks. Energy roared in like a stampeding lion! *Oh, my God!* The low back pain, the excruciating cramping, the abdominal swelling—all suddenly gone! I shuddered and wept uncontrollably. Those eyes! Those eyes had seen me and healed me!

Almost in disbelief, I stood up straight for the first time in over a decade. My spine felt strong and able to bear my weight. I wanted to dance, to scream, to fall down in worship! All I could do was stand there in awe, aware of only one thing—I was well!

I disappeared into the crowd, privately celebrating my incomprehensible healing. *My God had heard! My God had heard my prayer!*

I was so caught up in what had happened that I didn't notice the multitude had stopped. It suddenly grew eerily quiet, and from my view, I could see the top of someone's head turning around.

"Who touched me?" I heard a man ask.

Fear sliced through my heart. Surely he couldn't be talking about me. I didn't touch anybody. I only touched the hem of a garment. No one could have felt that.

One of his friends laughed a little. "Who touched you, Jesus? How can you ask that? Look at the crowd that surrounds you."

But as the crowd began to part, I could hear the man again ask: "Who touched me? I know that healing power has gone out from me."

Those eyes kept searching. Those eyes kept seeking. I was

immobilized. What was I going to do? If I came forward, everyone would know what my "issue" was. They would know about the secret things, the shameful things, the impure and defiled and isolated things. I had gone against the Law of Moses and made my way into the crowd. I was unclean, and I had defiled others. I would be beaten. How could I risk exposure? *You'll be humiliated,* I heard a voice inside say. *Stay hidden. Nobody needs to know about this. It can be between you and God. Don't expose yourself.*

Then it dawned on me that maybe he was angry. *Did I do something wrong? Maybe I defiled him! Oh, I can't tell him. I've got to run away. I need to hide!*

My legs buckled, this time not with pain, but with fear. Now I was immobilized, not for joy, but in terror. I wanted to move, but I couldn't. I wanted to run toward him and away from him at the same time. I knew I had to make a choice. It became clear it was time to come out of hiding, time to put away my pride. I decided to turn toward him. As I began to walk toward him, the closer I got, it was as if the strong grip of some unseen enemy began to tighten its hold. My entire being began to tremble. The voices inside shouted, *Run!* But I was tired of running and exhausted with hiding. Live or die, I wanted to just fall at his feet and rest.

The moment my hands hit the dirt by his side, my mouth began pouring out things I never knew were in my heart. I told him everything that had happened to me. I told him about the secret things I had done, the private things that had happened. I spilled my soul out and told the truth about the God-awful, should-never-have-been-done-to-me defilements I had endured. As I wept, it was as if streams of living water poured out from my eyes. The more I cried, the more I was cleansed.

What I thought was the most fearful thing I could do was becoming my greatest relief, even in front of a crowd of strangers.

For the first time in twelve years, somebody took my hand and lifted me up! For the first time in twelve years, I was touching someone, and they didn't recoil. I lost sight of everyone else. I didn't care. He was there! He had heard me!

Then he spoke: "Daughter..."

What? I was riveted.

He had just heard all the secret things I had done—the private sins and the sordid history of my life—and he called me, "Daughter?" Without a hint of accusation or ridicule, this Jesus was affirming my worth with just one word. With an utterly kind term of endearment, he was setting me back in my place in the family of God. In front of the entire town, he was re-establishing me in my community.

I could hardly believe it.

He continued: "Daughter, your faith—your belief in me and your choice to reach out to me—is what has saved and delivered you."

Was he saying that without my faith—my inching-forward little faith—his power would not have been demonstrated? I was astounded. I could hardly comprehend that he wasn't going to rebuke me for moving toward him in my unclean state. I was dumbfounded to discover he never intended to humiliate me when he had asked, "Who touched me?" He wanted to find me simply because he wanted to commend me!

I moved from condemnation to commendation with one simple phrase!

As he leaned toward me a little closer, my heart fluttered like a bird attempting to fly from its cage. With a strong urgency, he buried something deep in my spirit: "Go in peace ... withdraw into quietness. Be still and let your entire being rest from the turmoil you have endured."

Rest. I closed my eyes, barely able to remember the word. For all those years I had been required to be responsible for myself. No one else was.

But that wasn't all.

"Go," he said. "Live well; live blessed!"

A blessed life? The only blessings I ever knew had come a long time ago. But these words carried a hope with them, a sensation of peace that was so enticing I wanted to devour them.

"And be made whole from your plague," he said.

Plague. The word slapped me like a wet towel. That was the word the Romans use when they scourge a prisoner before crucifixion, whipping them bloody for being a criminal.

I looked at him with alarmed recognition as he again caught my eye.

Bloody?

It was as though his penetrating stare asked me a startling question: "Were you whipping yourself 'bloody'?"

He pressed into my soul more completely, more deeply than he had before, and his spirit said to my spirit:

"Daughter, you are freed, from here on out, from the unrelenting whipping of yourself as a criminal. I say to you, 'Stop beating yourself up! Go in peace. Be made whole from the suffering plague of self-hatred, guilt, and shame for whatever you have done that has contributed to your condition. Be freed now into the peace I have given you.'"

I was breathless. I could hardly take it in. But that wasn't all.

"And hear me in this," he said. "*Continue* to be whole."

My previously dulled senses were reverberating with life. With each word, I felt as if I was climbing out of a thick mountainous fog into the brilliant sun atop a soaring peak. I could hear and see everything clearly. Just as my body had been touched, so my mind was being renewed. It took me a moment to take it all in, but with each word he spoke, I came to better understand his meaning: this is a process! He said that I must do this part—continue to enter his rest and let his peace fill me. Just as my faith activated his power, my rest in him, my abiding in him, will maintain my healing.

It was more than I could have asked or hoped for.

It was then I realized that my breathing was no longer labored. I was at peace. I was wearing the same old rags, but I was no longer an old rag myself. I was standing up straight. I was looking others in the eye, and they were not backing away.

He smiled at me, enveloping me one last time with those astonishing eyes and turned around toward Jairus.

He had turned my mourning into dancing, and right there, in the dust, I twirled, just as David's sister would do, again and again and again.

REFLECTIONS

"A Woman and Her Issue"

1. This woman had an issue of blood. What's your issue?
    What are you internally bleeding from?
    Where is the hemorrhage in your heart?

2. The scripture records no name, no identity for this woman. We often name ourselves, or let others name us. Did she name herself:
    Unclean?
    Sick?
    Lonely?
    Estranged?
    Sexually unfulfilled?
    Isolated?
    Afraid?
    Rejected?
    Hopeless?
    Resourceless?
    Unable to contribute?
    Incapable of loving or being loved?
    Dying?

    What do you name yourself?

3. Does your "defilement" (whatever has caused you to feel unclean) urge you to stay out of any relationship or circumstance where you might be touched, physically or emotionally?

4. Does your injury cause you to reach out for touch in inappropriate ways to fill the vacuum of dark need in your heart?

5. If you're married, what injuries—physical, emotional, or spiritual—have kept you from intimacy with your spouse?

6. Are you hopeless because all the remedies you thought would work (getting married, having children, friends, enjoying health, career, success, or ministry) haven't fixed the hemorrhage inside your heart?

7. Are you disillusioned and bleeding over the fact that you've spent your energy, creativity, nurturing, and time on family or friends that now ignore you, or children who are on a track of rebellion and self-destruction?

8. Do you feel like you've been robbed of your youth, as this woman might have felt?

9. Do you feel that Jesus only takes time for the young?

10. You, with the sea of silver on your head, are you feeling spent, tossed aside, and destitute of purpose? God cares about the mature ones who have been overlooked, passed over, or disregarded because they're middle-aged or older! He cares about their "issues!"

To you, I can hear the Lord say something like this:

My dear friend, I have not forgotten you. I will call forth from your heart works of art that will be a treasure to me. I will not allow your lifeflow to bleed away with you, but I will redirect that flow into others who are desperate for their own touch from the Savior. I am giving you other children, children who have had no mother or father, no nurturing, and no kiss on the face; children who have languished, but children I am calling forth to life! Let me stop the hemorrhaging of your heart and show you purpose, for I have need of you. You are wanted. You are desired, and you are mine!

Dear ones, Jesus still heals the invisible ones. Jesus sees the humble and their secret requests, and doesn't ignore their private longing.

11. If you are young, what's your issue?

Proverbs 4:23 says, "Above all else, guard your heart, for out of it flows the issues of life. Have your youthful "affections" pushed you in the right or wrong direction?

12. Have you put appropriate boundaries on your feelings of love and desire in order to keep your heart protected, to keep it from bleeding and sustaining wounds too early in your life?

The Lord sees your issues! He calls you to protect that most private place—your heart—and oversee it with wisdom. He calls you to not give it or any part of you away to another prematurely because he resides there. He lives in your frame and your body is his home.

13. Are you so desperate for healing that you're willing to tell God and others the truth about your condition and come out of hiding? Are you willing to buck what's been your habit— victimization, isolation, even death—to press into the Lord's presence passing by you right now?

My friends, just like the woman with the issue, the Lord knows our fear. He sees the terror of exposure of our real selves. He sees the torment the enemy has used to keep us from intimacy with God and others, and he has already provided the healing for it. We must receive it and act on it by choosing to:

Come out of hiding by telling trustworthy, believing friends the truth of our experience. "Confess your sins, one to another, and pray for each other so that you may be healed" (James 5:16).

Forgive ourselves for the sins we've committed against others and ourselves. Here's a sample prayer:

> Father, I confess the sins I've committed against myself (name them), and I confess my sinful-reactions against those who have hurt me (name them). In my heart I confess the sins I've committed against You, and I acknowledge my need for a Savior who came in the flesh to take upon Himself the penalty for my sin. I choose to accept that Savior's phenomenal love for me, and I ask Jesus, the Christ, to take up residence in my life that I may know the abundance of life he intends to bring me. I receive his Holy Spirit into my being, and I choose to forgive myself and those who have hurt me, and receive your wonderful washing, your new beginnings, and your forgiveness.
>
> I open my mouth to receive your breath. Resuscitate me, Father. Call me to life. Wherever the suffering woman exists, Lord, heal me.
>
> Wherever the flow of life has been drained from me, heal me.
>
> Wherever my hopes for change have been annihilated, heal me.
>
> Wherever my creativity has been discharged from me without it being fully realized, heal me of my disappointment and disillusionment.
>
> Wherever my sexuality has been robbed from me, heal me.

Wherever my body has required so much energy just to survive, heal me.

Wherever my soul has longed for friendship and I have been ostracized, ignored, or just been invisible, heal me.

Wherever my attitudes about myself have been critical, hate-filled, or have been without self-care, heal me.

Wherever I have been isolated from or rejected by my spouse, heal me.

Wherever I have looked for you to meet me, and I felt like you passed me by, reach out your hand, and heal me.

Thank you, Father.
Amen.

If you confess with your mouth that Jesus is Lord and believe in your heart that God raised him from the dead, you will be saved. For it is by believing in your heart that you are made right with God, and it is by confessing with your mouth that you are saved" (Romans 10:9-10 NLT).

Chapter Two

CLEANING JAIRUS' HOUSE

Luke 8:40-52

We had been awake all night with our daughter, Neriah. Her breathing had become more and more erratic, and her skin had changed to the color of the ash we throw on our heads when we're in mourning.

There are no words to describe the terror of watching your child die.

All the physicians, all the prayers—nothing had worked to interrupt the decay invading the life of our little one. Nothing. We were despondent.

My wife Hanniel and I were sitting next to Neriah's bed, too numb to cry. I looked across the palette at the woman I'd married, remembering how she had been so many years ago. Given her fixation with Neriah these last several months, it was hard to imagine that, eleven years ago, she had not really wanted a baby. Hanniel had been a merchant of cloth. Her giftedness had been in buying and selling, and she always made a handsome profit. She loved beautiful things, and she thrived on looking important. When she found out she was due with child, something in her died, and she went into a silent mourning about the loss of her independent life.

I could understand that. Being the overseer of the synagogue here in Capernaum, my congregation was like my child. I loved the people in it as my own. I wasn't sure that I wanted a child, either. So much bother. But wonder of wonders, God looked into our comfortable nest and gave us this little chirp of life!

As Neriah grew up, she would often want to sit on my lap, or lean against Hanniel's breast, and something in Hanniel and I began to shift. We slowly began to draw close as a family. Just this last year, I'd begun to see the beginnings of womanhood in her, and I suddenly longed for the early years to return when I might have thrown her up in the air, held her fat baby fingers in my palm, or carried her on my strong shoulders. She had become the joy of our lives.

As I looked at Neriah and Hanniel in the dim candlelight, I could hardly tell which one was dying more. It seemed that, instead of our giving life to our child, she had given it to us. And now that life was seeping out of all three of us with each labored breath she took.

An anxious banging on the door jarred my thoughts.

My legs felt so weak from fear that I could hardly rise and make it to the door. Our neighbor, Jachan, had come to bring us news. Flushed, breathless with excitement, he began speaking so fast I almost couldn't understand him.

"Jesus has come!" he said. "He's on the beach near the market! Come! Bring your child! Bring her to the Lord!"

My pulse quickened. "The Lord?" I asked.

I had heard and seen this carpenter before. My co-workers, the Pharisees, had sneered at him in mockery during several of our meals together, and I had joined in on some of their laughter. Who in their right mind would believe the Messiah

18

would come in such a package? They spat when they said his name and called him a blasphemer.

I had to admit, however, that he did have a certain presence. I remembered that day in the synagogue when he stood up and read from the prophet Isaiah. His manner was commanding without being intimidating. He spoke with a loving and yet restrained power in his voice that held me at attention, creating in me a longing for what he was saying. I wanted to hear more, to think more—maybe to be more like him—but my position was one of responsibility. If I validated this man to my congregation, and he was a fake, I might lead them astray. I also might look like a fool. In my position, I couldn't risk either one.

And yet, I was intrigued by the miracles.

A woman three homes away had a lump in her neck that the physicians could not heal. She came to show me the place where it had once been, saying "the Messiah" had healed her. When I asked her who the Messiah was, she said, "Jesus of Nazareth."

I inspected her neck. It was true. The goiter was gone.

There was also an old man named Chebar who had limped for years on his right hip, which was aggravated each time he stood up straight. He came running back into town the afternoon he had seen Jesus, rejoicing that he was pain-free and without a limp.

And then there had been Giddel, the young man in my congregation whose head hurt so fiercely from an accident he would scream in agony. Just yesterday I had seen him, clear-eyed and exuberant over being without pain for five months.

My daughter's gasping for air drew my thinking back to reality, and I looked helplessly at Jachan.

"She's getting worse, Jairus," he whispered as he craned his neck toward the room to listen.

My mind was fighting to stay rational. *Could I . . . ?* No, I couldn't take her down there. I would be laughed at. Besides, Hanniel would hurt me before she let me take her to a simple carpenter who performs miracles.

I shook my head at Jachan. "We cannot come," I whispered to my friend.

Jachan's face dropped with disappointment, but he touched my shoulder to console me, nodding in understanding.

I closed the door and leaned my back against it. I was too numb to think. The light from the window fell onto the dirt floor. I gazed at it as if in a dream and watched it begin to glow, as if it were just coming out from behind the clouds.

My mind spun back to when Jesus read the passage from Isaiah in our synagogue: "To comfort all who mourn, and provide for those who grieve in Zion; to release the oppressed, to proclaim the year of the Lord's favor." He had read the verses with a resonance and what seemed like a personal knowing in his voice.

Strange coming from such a young man, I had thought.

Suddenly, just then, I remembered the last part of what he'd said. He had rolled up the scroll, set it down, and looked out on the worshipping faces that day, declaring: "Today this scripture is fulfilled in your hearing."

Oh, my good Jehovah! Suddenly, I began to question my own thinking. I remembered that while I was in his presence, I found myself profoundly alive with a peculiar joy that I had never before felt!

I walked around the room, holding my head. *Was this possible? Could he be the Son of God?*

My mind raced through the words in Isaiah, the Psalms, and all the other scriptures that predicted the Messiah's coming.

Isaiah 9: Galilee would be the first area of his ministry.

Isaiah 35: Messiah would perform miracles.

Jeremiah 23: Messiah would be called "The Lord."

Those, and many others that flooded my thoughts, all began to fall into place! *Could he be . . . could he be the One who was to come?* The warm light falling through the window made my head grow hot. Did I just want to believe in him because of my desperation? I sank to my knees, my head in the dust. *Oh, my God Jehovah! Could I actually be alive at the time of his coming? Would this miracle of miracles be possible, and would he come today?* I felt delirious with the idea.

A vigorous, unexpected energy swept through my being. My mind went completely still, and something in me began to surge with anticipation.

Yes, yes, he could be our Messiah! Jesus could be the Messiah!

Without thinking, my hands went up into the air, and I began to dance the dance of Hebrew celebration. An unworldly joy swept through my body and, before I knew it, I was laughing out loud . . . until my exhilaration was ripped in half by my wife's shrill scream. I raced for Neriah. When I reached the doorway, her eyes were rolling into the back of her head, and she was jerking involuntarily up and down, up and down. She was biting her tongue so hard it was bleeding.

Hanniel was hysterical, screaming, "She's convulsing! She's convulsing! She's going to die!"

I couldn't stand to watch anymore. I turned my head away, listening as her body lay thumping, thumping against the bed, and the gagging noises came, and the . . . oh, no more. *No more!*

I ran out of the house dressed in nothing more than a tunic. My head was swimming. My eyes couldn't focus. The only thing I could see was his face. Messiah or not, blasphemer or not, I would not let my child die if I could do anything about it!

My furious running grew stronger with each breath I took. People from the temple watched me sweep by them, choking back my tears, devoid of my elegant rabbinical robes. I didn't care. I only knew I had to find him. I only knew that if I could just get him to come and put his strong hand on my daughter, that strange knowing, that authoritative power that came out of him when he read the book, would come out of him toward her! I ran with all my might.

The thought was constant: *Just ask him, and he will come.*

When I saw Jesus on the shore of the Sea of Galilee, he was bending over talking with a child about Neriah's age. I took it as a sign. I ran into the crowd, and when the people saw who I was, they parted to make way for me. Jesus stood up straight and tilted his head. Even then I saw an understanding on his face, the knowing that he knew what I needed. I fell down into the sticky mud, sweat pouring down my face, barely covered in the shell of my garment. I held onto his knees, sobbing without words, broken by the pain of my deepest fear.

Somehow I choked it out: "My child. Come. Put your hands on her. She will be healed and live."

I saw in his eyes the kind of glistening light that I'd seen on the sea at daybreak.

"I will come," he said with a confident face. "I will come."

He helped me up, and when he touched me, I don't know how to explain it, but I lost all fatigue. My whole frame was invigorated. My heart leapt with hope! If he would come, I knew my daughter would be healed!

We started toward my home with what felt like a mass of bodies, some cheering, all of them pressing, calling his name, "Jesus! Jesus!"

Some that surrounded him must have been angry that he was coming with me since they had been there first. They began to shove and push the crowd, creating a death trap inside the massive throng, so much so that Jesus had to climb up on someone's shoulders just to catch his breath.

When he got down, we started toward my house, but it was then that the interruption occurred.

Without warning, Jesus just stopped! I saw him turn around with searching eyes, asking what seemed like a silly question: "Who touched me?"

I stood back, incredulous that given the need at hand, Jesus let himself become distracted! I didn't know what to do to get him moving again. Until today, I had always been the one in control. I had always stayed focused. If there was a job, I finished it. If I gave my word, I followed through. I prided myself on being punctual, responsible, trustworthy. After all, people depended on me.

Having regained some of my rabbinical composure, I tried to remain patient with Jesus, thinking surely he would pat the woman on the head and tell her to come back another day. Surely her ten- or twelve-year whatever-it-happened-to-be was not nearly as important as my need.

The older woman began to say her piece, tell him about her past, cried a little, and then I thought, *Good, she's done.* Then she started wailing. She told him every single little detail about what had hurt her as he listened and gently held her hand.

I started pacing. I ran my fingers through my hair time and time again. I was agitated at first, then I became irritated, and finally I was infuriated!

Don't you get it that my baby is dying? I internally screamed. *What's more important than that? This woman is old! She's lived her life! Why are you staying here? You said you'd come with me!*

I kept looking toward my house, desperately wondering what was going on behind the thick mud walls.

After what seemed like hours to my frantic thinking, Jesus

said to the woman, "Go in peace and be freed from your plague." Just then two of my wife's cousins quietly pushed through the crowd. I could tell by the look on their faces what their news was. I started to shake my head. *No! No!* They took my arms, holding onto me to keep me from falling.

They whispered in my left ear: "Jairus, your daughter is dead. No need to bother the teacher anymore."

I think my body began to shake. I could feel myself sinking into an abyss of terrifying black grief. We were too late. He had taken time for someone else, and now...

I started to collapse.

Just then, Jesus saw me. He grabbed me and swung me to the side, out of the grasp of my relatives. He looked me directly in the eye.

"Fear not," he said. "Just believe."

"Fear not?"

I felt like saying, *What do you mean, 'Fear not? Just believe?' My daughter is dead!"*

"Fear not. Just believe," he quietly repeated.

I wanted to throw it in his face. *What do you mean, "Just believe?" Do you think believing is easy? Look at what's real! Get a grip, Jesus! My daughter is dead! These are the facts. Why didn't you do what you promised to do? If you had only come quickly, she would not have died!*

In that split second, I suddenly realized I was internally wrestling with two sets of voices. One said, "The circumstances are clear—all is lost. Hope is gone. I put my trust in you and you failed me." On the other side, a stalwart voice with a solid-as-an-oak demeanor that clipped the other one and overruled it like a judge in a trial said: "Do not be afraid. Only believe. Do not be frightened or alarmed, but be in awe and reverence. Entrust yourself to me. Don't be afraid that I seem to be coming when things look too late. Believe that I know exactly what I'm doing."

I was too much in a stupor to realize the powerful principle he was teaching me. At that point in my spiraling pain, through an event that would change the course of my life forever, Jesus was pulling me up by the tunic, saying: "Before the enemy of your soul can plant a new set of beliefs in your thinking, I am here to intercept it. Ignore any voice other than mine."

I heard him, but it didn't sink in. I heard him, but I had to think. Ignore any voice other than yours? Ignore what seems to be my reality for a reality that only you see? *God, help my faith!* But I recognized I had no choice. Either I was going to sink into the hell of my despair, or I would listen and obey him.

Something beyond my human capacity took over. My weak faith suddenly expanded within me, and a force greater than my puny ability overtook my mind. Something compelled me to believe him. And somehow, I did.

It would have been one thing if Jesus had said, "Fear not, just believe," and remained there to comfort me. But Jesus proceeded to walk with me directly toward the place of my greatest heartache. Part of me, naturally, wanted to go and be with my family, believing that Jesus was right and my daughter would be healed. But the other part of me resisted having to face seeing my child dead. I couldn't bear the thought of it. But that's exactly where Jesus steered me—to face everything I dreaded.

He seemed to read my thoughts. Again he said: "Don't be afraid, Jairus. Trust me."

It was the longest walk I've ever made. I felt schizophrenic, still struggling with the human reasoning that said everything was lost. I didn't want to confront my inconsolable wife. I didn't want to gaze at the one who had become the joy of my life—my only child—in an ashen, lifeless heap on the bed.

On the other hand, I couldn't deny a peculiar growing

hope burning in my chest, an unnatural peace and strange optimism that grew stronger with every step I took with Jesus.

I had the choice. I took it. I chose to keep up with the determined purpose in Jesus' pace to keep myself from sinking into a pit of despair.

On the way, he whispered to me: "We do not sorrow as those who have no hope."

By the time we got to my house there was pandemonium everywhere—weeping, chest pounding, and wailing from every quarter. Neighbors, along with our daughter's playmates, were stacked like limp fish against our exterior wall, soaked in tears. A couple of them hung on my arms as I approached the entrance, almost gagging in their frantic grief. A few women from the village let out long, mournful shrieks and held them without taking a breath until they faded away in quiet, painful sobs.

Someone had already hired some professional mourners, men and women I didn't know, who tore their outer clothing, hid their chin beneath their tunics, and wailed loudly while throwing dust and ashes over their heads. But it was the dreadful melancholic dirge the minstrels played that filled my lungs with the internal heaviness of an approaching monsoon.

When I made my way through the door, my wife collapsed into my chest with heavy sobs. My whole body shook, absorbing her sorrow in wave after wave of hysterical tears.

Just then, the room quieted as thirteen odd-looking, unkempt strangers followed me into our home. I looked around, aware of how out of place they looked compared to the neatly dressed upper-crust strata of society which I usually befriended.

Our relatives stopped their frenetic weeping and stared at me incredulously, as if I had dared to bring strangers into the mouth of our family tomb.

Jesus surveyed the crowd curiously, then suddenly cleared his throat and asked, "Why all this commotion and wailing? The child is not dead; she's just asleep."

I swung around to look at him. I had had enough shocks for one morning! *What was this stranger doing? What was I doing with this stranger?*

My wife was so wide-eyed I wasn't sure how to read her, but beyond her I could see the nostrils on her father's face flaring like a trumpet preparing to blare.

With Jesus' unthinkable declaration, a flood of palpable scorn poured from the room where my relatives sat.

"What did you say?" yelled my red-eyed sister-in-law with a contemptuous scowl. "Are you mocking us in our grief?"

"How dare you allow this nobody to enter your own house and ridicule us!" my brother accused me.

Some Pharisee associates who were standing in the corner looked at Jesus and then quickly at me. I couldn't speak, so they thought I was agreeing with him. And I guess I was! In that moment, I made a conscious choice to agree with the one who said there was life in my daughter, rather than agree with the ones who spoke about her death. I decided I would rather watch what he was doing and do it, than shrink back and do nothing at all!

"You're going to give this man authority over your own home?" my relatives demanded.

"Think about your position! You're going to look like a fool! Don't you know this is going to cost you with us?" the Pharisees hissed.

The wailing of the mourners increased, escalating the tangible tension.

Jesus stood in the middle of the room, surveying the myriad of faces. His manner was almost defiant, but his face was full of hope.

Finally, my brothers, who had eaten their fill of this intruder, started to get up to throw him out. But who would have guessed—Jesus disarmed them and threw them out! He ran them right out the door.

I looked at my wife in disbelief. *What was happening?*

An instant later, Jesus looked at the women in the family who were wailing uncontrollably, their arms flapping like chickens at the slaughter. He confronted them one by one and ordered them out of the house. Gulping back their sobs, each one wilted under his powerful gaze and fled outside. Those who were left—the snickering Pharisees, the doleful musicians, and the professional mourners—looked like someone had physically asssaulted them and slunk out into the street.

Had Jesus lost his mind? Had I?

Jesus looked at me as if he were waiting for my next move. Almost like an exclamation point, I ran over and bolted the door shut. To my complete surprise, I broke out in laughter! *Was I going out of my mind?*

Jesus coughed at the dust stirred up in the room and wiped it from his eyes as he smiled at me. He had swept out anyone who would have sabotaged the fullness of believing faith in our home. He had used the authority I gave him to clean my house of all the voices that agreed with anything that had to do with death.

Jesus walked over to my stupefied wife, took her gently by the elbow, and guided her along with his friends, Peter, James and John, into the candlelit room where Neriah was lying.

He had set the scene for the greatest display of his power, coupled with our faith, ever to be seen.

"She is not dead," he reminded us, calmly. "She is just asleep."

REFLECTIONS

"Cleaning Jairus' House"

1. Do you feel, as Jairus might have, that Jesus says he wants to heal you, but there are so many delays you're becoming frustrated, afraid, or hopeless?

2. Do you wonder why other people seem to get priority over you?

3. What kind of losses are you grieving?

4. What are the voices saying in your head?
   "My needs don't matter?"
   "I have no hope for my children because they're too
      far gone?"
   "I don't have the kind of faith that gets results?"
   "I can't afford to follow him. My family or my community
      wouldn't understand."
   "I want to be healed, but if I go up and ask, I'll look like a
      fool and be embarrassed."

5. When what you have most feared has happened, have you preferred to steer away from the pain rather than confront it as Jesus helped Jairus do?

6. Do you have a "fear of feeling?"

7. Where does fear come from? Who is the author of it?

8. Jairus gave Jesus the authority to clean out all of his

sneering, disdainful relatives. He chose to put his hope in Jesus' power rather than appease the friends who wanted to ridicule his faith. Jairus made a choice to risk ostracizing his family and friends rather than miss out on the intervention of God in his life. He had the courage to prefer faith over the familiar. Many of these people may have been Pharisees, people who were respected in the temple, people who had celebrity, influence, and wealth. Some of them may have been his superiors, and I'm sure there were several offended, incredulous relatives. Jairus did not indulge them. He trusted Jesus' call and gave Jesus permission to do what he needed to do, regardless of what it would cost him relationally.

9. Is there a snickering Pharisee inside you—a part of you that is judgmental, hypocritical, or proud as you survey the landscape of others lives?

10. Like Jairus, do you feel you have to perform up to the expectations of others or they will ostracize you, and you'll be out of their favor?

11. Whose opinions matter most to you? Why?

When calamity broadsides us, we often feel we have a right to express our indignations, accusations, and entitlements to "life, liberty and the pursuit of happiness!" Sometimes we blame others, sometimes ourselves, sometimes God. Grieving our losses is crucial to our inner health, ("Blessed are those who mourn, for they will be comforted." Matt. 5:4), but we are not entitled to mock God in the process.

In the Old Testament, David vented his questions to God: "I say to God, my rock: 'Why must I go about mourning, oppressed by the enemy?'" (Ps. 42:9) He felt the confusions, pain and losses, but he expressed them rightly, realizing that God was his sure foundation. He believed in God's good will, even through the pain of his suffering.

In the book of Job, within a two-day period, Job lost ten children, his health, and his wealth. He endured harassment, indictments, and accusations from the mouths of his wife and friends. But listen to this verse in Job 1:22: "In all this, Job did not sin by charging God with wrongdoing."

My friend, it's imperative that we grieve rightly, but that we do not ever accuse God of wrongdoing. Tell God the truth of what you feel with all the authenticity you have. Be real, be vocal, be honest even if you perceive that it's he that has caused or allowed your agony, and then choose to trust him at the end with a prayer of worship. It will help you become ready for what it is he wants to do next: raise something to life from the death of your suffering.

Chapter Three

NOT DEAD, JUST ASLEEP

Luke 8:53-56

The room was musty and dimly lit by flickering lamps positioned on each side of Neriah's body. My daughter's thick black hair had fallen off the end of the bed, and it was disheveled from the violent forces that had taken the life from her.

This was the first time I had seen her. Everything inside me clamored for hope.

Maybe she really is just asleep. Maybe what he says is true. Has anybody listened to her breathing?

I didn't ask these questions out loud, but instead I shouted them inside my brain, praying, begging, and hoping against hope that she was only asleep.

But she was not. The outline along her lips was beginning to show a purplish hue, contrasting with the beige-grey pallor that had enveloped her face. Her hands were swollen. Dried blood was hanging from the corner of her mouth. The eyes that had danced with merriment in our home were a quarter opened, vacant and blank, like a bludgeoned blackbird. Upon seeing her, my throat began to close, and I had a hard time breathing. I gasped, perhaps to help her breathe again, but I wept instead. I wasn't sure if I might die from the massive weight I felt on my chest.

"Do not fear. Only believe."

One of Jesus' friends put two fingers in front of her nose to check for any breathing. He shook his head at the others and withdrew his hand. Jesus didn't watch. He kept his gaze steadily on my daughter, walking around her bed like an eagle scouting a place to land. The wings of his outer robe opened like feathers, and the tassels began to dance in a syncopated rhythm, as if they heard singing from a faraway place.

I saw that he was breathing in through his nose, then out through his mouth; in through his nose, out through his mouth. It reminded me of the ancient Scripture: "God breathed into his nostrils the breath of life, and man became a living soul." As long as I watched him, my inner scream quieted. As long as my eyes remained on him, the candles seemed to give more light.

My wife, who had been too spent to react, walked from the shadows of the room toward the light and held my hand. I wondered what she had been thinking. She would never have permitted a stranger to enter her home at such a time as this. Yet from the moment of his entrance, she acquiesced to his command. Her attention was focused upon him. She bore no suspicion and exhibited no qualms. For once in her life, her tongue was silent. As Jesus walked around her bed, the graying hair on Hanniel's head seemed to turn the color of our daughter's, shining and youthful. I blinked, thinking it was my imagination.

Jesus' manner and face seemed to create an atmosphere that was renewing, an atmosphere that was irresistible.

My eyes moved from him to my daughter. For the first time I realized how mature she had gotten. Her chubby frame had slendered into the beauty of a willow tree. I had never noticed that her feet had grown into the same size as Hanniel's, but there on the bed I saw she was wearing her mother's sandals. It was at that moment that Hanniel reached over and gave our daughter a ring from her own finger. It was the ring her mother had given her at age twelve, the ring that would have welcomed our child into womanhood at her bat mitzvah on her birthday. Was this a signal to Jesus that she believed she would celebrate Neriah's next birthday?

Hanniel looked me in the eye, but what surprised me was that the tears welling up were not laced with grief. They were brimming with a profound new energy, a hope that I had not seen in her face since the time of our engagement. Something was calling her to life, and she was calling back! I pulled her toward me. Our bodies trembled as we stood together, caught up in a strange internal wind that filled us with an indefinable expectation.

Jesus looked at us and then at Neriah with a gaze that might have parted waters. Those eyes seemed to penetrate past the stained cloth of her gown and directly encounter her heart. The expression on his face changed every few seconds, as if he were confronting a bull in a pen, and he was determined to win. He looked defiant, radiant, compassionate, and conquering. He was exploding with love and a quiet power. The combination of his face, his figure, and his fluidity created a living poem around the room.

Without knowing it, all of us began to breathe at the same time and in the same way. All of us were drawn into the rhythm of his person—penetrated with a presence that was as electrifying as lightening, and as quiet as a prayer.

Jesus walked over to Neriah's side. As if anticipating his next gesture, my wife and I removed the candles beside her, but the light didn't flicker or fade. It intensified around him.

I stood beside him as a comrade, as a disciple, and my spirit cried out to his spirit, "I believe in you!"

Jesus reached out to take our daughter by the hand. He took a deep, extended breath in, and vehemently commanded: "Talitha Koum—Little girl, I say to you, arise!"

A blast of air shot through Neriah's lungs. Her chest cavity, covered by tender pubescent breasts, was extended into the fullness of a womanly figure. Her mouth opened wide, drinking in the resuscitating life-breath that ran like a thoroughbred throughout her frame. The quarter-moon slits of her eyes jerked open with a vibrancy and color that made us all gasp, all of us except Jesus.

Hanniel cried out in astonished disbelief and belief! Our daughter blinked twice, and quite naturally turned her beautiful head toward Jesus. Without any visible strain, she lifted her body off the bed, put her feet on the floor, and stood up next to the Messiah in perfect obedience, radiantly alive!

My wife collapsed into the Savior, leaning against our child breast to breast. I fell to the floor, my hands on each of their feet, sobbing without restraint. We had no words—only tears, joyous tears. I couldn't see the others, but I could hear their astonishment. The singing, the worship, the sacred prayer that arose—it was as if we were in the heaven we speak about going to.

The Messiah took Neriah in his arms, and embraced her like I had never known how to do. He whispered in her ear this ancient poem of King Solomon's:

Not Dead, Just Asleep

Arise, my darling,
My beautiful one and come with me.
See, the winter is past
The rains are over and gone.
Flowers appear on the earth
The season of singing has come.
The cooing of doves
Is heard in our land.
The fig tree forms its early fruit,
The blossoming vines spread their fragrance.
Arise, come, my darling,
My beautiful one, come with me.

REFLECTIONS

"Not Dead. Just Asleep."

In the scriptural passage of this story, Jesus "went in where the child was" (Luke 8:53-56). He walked into her circumstance and took her by the hand. Even in her frozen, slumbering spirit, he met her.

1. Do you feel as if you're "asleep" and can't "wake up"?

2. Do you understand what it's like to be unable to make any efforts to move toward God?

3. Are you crying out to him to come and meet you?

4. In the context of these interwoven stories, Jesus healed the suffering woman before he raised the dead little girl. Are you willing to allow him to touch and heal the present-day woman, which may then awaken and call to life the long-lost little girl?

5. Within himself, Jairus didn't have what it took to call his daughter to life. Did your Dad?

Without Jairus' choice to act, his daughter would never have met the Master. Jairus' action changed the course of his family's bloodline and their spiritual heritage!

Our earthly fathers have all failed us in one way or another, but God the Father wants to send the blast of his breath into our souls to breathe into us the breath of life. He will have his daughters and sons called forth to life! He is a consistent, trustworthy, safe father, able to nourish us and bring us the affection we need!

As with Jairus' daughter, the Lord Jesus says to us: "Talitha Koum! Little one, I say to you, arise! Collect your faculties and wake up! Arise from lying on your bed of inactivity and ruin! Awaken from obscurity! Come forth from your non-existence!"

Father, we pray that you come and call to life in us what our earthly fathers could not. We ask you that you send the breath of your spirit into our souls and fill every place with the power of your life and love. Call forth our capacity to:

> Play
> Dream
> Have friends
> Fall in love
> Engage with life
> Give birth
> Become mature
> Be authentic
> Reproduce
> Be creative
> Have hope
> Be passionate
> Give and receive love
> Laugh
> Be beautiful
> Nurture
> Trust
> Dance.

Father, show us where we have agreed with anything that would cause us to want to give up on life. We now renounce any agreement we have made with those forms of death in any capacity, and we choose life with you! Awaken us from the slumbering stupor of lifelessness into the fullness of our destiny! Amen.

Chapter Four

FREE TO JUST BE

Luke 10:38-42

Iawoke with familiar knots in my shoulders, pinching not only my physical, but also my emotional nerves. The sleep I had hoped would rest my mind had only temporarily kept at bay all that I needed to accomplish that day. Like the centurion officers who roamed our hillsides, duty seemed to command my attention every waking hour.

Internally, I was held hostage by my heavy responsibilities—my duty to take care of the household, to see that the servants were accountable, and to take care of my siblings, Mary and Lazarus. I am Martha, the oldest. That's always the job of the oldest.

I rubbed my head to help the blood circulate and sat up to stretch my neck from side to side.

So much to do. So little time.

I glanced at my sister across the room on her mat, her long hair layered like a raven's wing across her fit, but feminine arm. Her porcelain face bore little resemblance to my own. There seemed to be no frown lines, no little wrinkles around her mouth that would betray any internal worries.

How can she be so content? I wondered.

I sighed, wishing I could be jealous of somebody that lovely, but I couldn't. Despite her lack of self-discipline and her delight in dreaming her days away, I couldn't help but love the heart that moved her with such grace to embrace the poor or spend hours listening to widows in their grief. We each have our gifts, I decided. She had hers; I had mine, but why was mine so all-consuming? I never had time to dawdle and no time to think, not with all there was to do.

I looked at myself in the large copper mirror and noticed that my face was peppered with spots that seemed to have grown more intense as I aged. I stood sideways and saw that my nose appeared to protrude worse than I'd feared, and my hips had expanded to a matronly girth. With all I beheld in the mirror, I let out a long sigh like the noise of the blacksmith's black bellows. The one saving grace for my looks was that, secretly, I liked the color of my eyes. They had a tint of olive, unlike those of Lazarus or Mary, whose eyes were typical of our Jewishness—shiny brown, large, and round. Mine had flair, I decided. I thanked my father, God rest his soul, who had told me he had willed me his eyes when I was young.

"If the oldest must bear the brunt, they should also bear the blessing," he had said.

It had been the one compliment he had given me. For when my two younger siblings came along, his affirmations were always focused on them. They needed him more. At least that's what I told myself.

Father had died two decades earlier when he was about Lazarus' age. I cared for him when he was sick because Mother was not up to it. He suffered for several weeks after the physicians had exhausted their limited knowledge about his condition. The night he died, I think Mother's heart died, too. Mercifully, her body caught up with her heart only ten days later.

I smiled sadly and sucked in a deep breath. I missed them so, but there was no time to feel that now.

Mary stirred for a moment as I brushed my long brown hair. When I lowered my eyes to tie it high behind my head, I noticed the water jar was empty again. *Of course. What should I expect?* I threw a glance in Mary's direction and thought about waking her to fill it. As usual I knew she'd agree and just turn over and fall back asleep.

You do everything anyway. You ought to be used to it by now, a voice inside reminded me. The spasms in my shoulders twitched in angry agreement.

As I walked toward the stairs, I deliberated whether I should help harvest the barley or fix the cracked olive oil pot. I made a mental note to ask Lazarus to help me as I went down to the main room of our home, but surprisingly, he was already up stoking the fire. He smiled sheepishly at me and handed me a brewed cup of leaves he'd been saving.

"I heard you sneeze last night. I thought you might like this. Don't eat the herb. It's bitter. Just drink the tea."

I laughed a little, embarrassed by being surprised to see him, and thanked him. I wasn't used to being taken care of. He broke off a piece of cardamom bread and handed it to me. We sat wordlessly for a minute by the fire, huddling against the morning chill. The flickering fire highlighted the dark rust tones in his wavy hair. For the first time, I noticed his features were chiseled in an almost perfect fusion of our parents— Mother's eyes, nose and smile along with Father's cheekbone, ears, and forehead. Physically, I knew he wasn't as strong as others his age, but his mind could dazzle any challenger with a quick and witty retort.

An almost overwhelming burst of joy rose in my throat as I sat there. I wanted to throw my arms around him and tell him how much I loved him, how I adored him for his integrity, his kindness, and his skill as a merchant. But, I didn't. As quickly as it came, I swallowed, and it receded. No time for foolishness.

I realized right then that I never was very good at touching, talking, or even understanding people. Mary and Lazarus always seemed to have known how. They were constantly talking together, dreaming about the future, or discussing prophecies about the Messiah and his appearing. Secretly, I wished I could be more like them, more able to just enjoy life, but in my pride I had never shared that with them.

Lazarus interrupted my thoughts. "Martha, I've heard there's a man who people are calling 'the Christ.'" The tenor of his voice heightened a little and an intensity came over his face.

"He's been traveling throughout Judea and Galilee, and miracles are happening wherever he goes! Up north in Capernaum, he even raised a little girl from the dead!"

Lazarus got up and started pacing in circles, gesturing excitedly.

"He teaches amazing stories! His words make people hungry for more. Mary and I want to see him. Do you want to go with us?"

Oh, I thought secretly, *There they go, the two of them again.*

I cleared my throat. "The, uh, hummus needs…" I got up and started moving somewhat speedily toward the kitchen. I could see his face fall into a sad but polite half-smile.

"It's okay," I said with just the slightest whine. "You two go. I'll stay and take care of things here. Have a good time."

I did, however, pat his shoulder on the way to the kitchen.

As I left the room, I felt like a cold draft had blown by me, and instead of being warmed and filled, I felt like I'd just eaten the bitter herb.

Our house was very near the road Jews traveled on the way to Jerusalem. Later that afternoon while we were all in the field, we saw a band of travelers raising an unusual amount of dust. Dust always gets my attention.

"How dare those people make such a commotion!" I spewed at Mary.

Mary and Lazarus hardly heard me. They dropped their tools and began to walk to see who was coming. Was it a Roman governor? Could it be the new rabbi who was coming to Bethany?

Must be a traveling minstrel, I thought. *There go all the children.*

But this was no band of musicians. I couldn't help but follow Mary and Lazarus toward the road as they approached.

We could see that a man in the middle of the group stopped walking as a young mother brought an injured child to him. Both the boy's legs were twisted and deformed, dangling awkwardly from his thin hips. We could hear her begging the man in a loud voice: "Heal him! Please heal my child!" Then, with his authoritative, muscular hand, the man reached out.

My good Jehovah! The child's legs jerked up and flew around! He kicked them high and then to the side, his deformity obviously gone! When his mother put him on the ground, he began jumping up and down, running, twisting, and leaping into the air. His legs were now fully developed. He danced around and jumped into the man's arms, right in front of my house!

My stomach bolted into my chest, and my heart was thumping wildly. *Did I just see...? Who could this be?* I turned toward Mary and Lazarus but they had already started running to the road. I ran, too!

Was this the One who was to come?

The jubilation of the miracle sent a crackle of euphoria throughout the growing crowd. An exuberant chant began. "Blessed is He who comes in the name of the Lord!" The words reverberated in my aging ears, and I wondered for a moment if my own hearing had improved.

This young healer had a smile as lively as a bubbling brook. He looked up as we made our way into the throng, greeting all three of us as if we had been his friends all our lives. I stumbled over my greeting, entranced by the sense of his presence, which felt warm and cool at the same time. He greeted me and held my hands, then curiously lifted his eyes to see where we lived.

Instinctively, I mumbled: "Your robe and feet are..." I surveyed his face. "You're hungry? Yes, I can tell you are! Come! Come to our house. Come and dine! Come with your friends, all of them. Come and refresh yourselves!"

He smiled broadly, pleased at my invitation.

"Yes, your house. Yes. Let us go, brothers!"

An inner squeal leapt from my throat, much to my adult surprise. Why was I so beside myself?

But then I started counting. Four, eight . . . thirteen? Thirteen hungry men, plus the three of us for dinner? What had I done?

"Mary! Set the table!" I called out when we reached the house. "Don't forget Father's special cups! We must gather the greens from the garden, and lentil soup should help fill some of those bellies!" I laughed.

"And Lazarus," I yelled, cupping my hands around my mouth, "Don't forget to serve the pomegranate wine!" How I thanked God above we had dressed a lamb for dinner!

My head was soon sweat-soaked from the steam rising over several pots. The figs, dates, and melons had been cut and arranged beautifully with a sprout of jasmine in the middle. I stirred the hummus and threw in a little extra dill and some pine nuts to give it added crunch, and managed to warm the unleavened bread so it had the toasty edge that always elicited a compliment.

It seemed almost providential that Jesus and his men would have come that day. Lentils have to be soaked for several hours before cooking, and I had put them in water early that morning, thinking I would make a pot for the week's noon meals. A special honey glaze simmered near the oven where the raisin cakes were baking, and as I checked on them, I was pleased that I had remembered to add a touch of cinnamon.

The house was aromatic, more filled with life than I could recall, and while I cooked, I overheard stories from the other room of what the Master had said and done—how 72 of his disciples had been sent out, and that even demons submitted to them in his name! For a moment I forgot about the preparations. *How could this be? Who was this man resting in my home?*

One disciple, Bartholomew, told a story of Jesus feeding 5,000 people with . . . what was it . . . five loaves and two fish? Blind children and deaf women were healed, and on top of that, lepers were cured! I couldn't resist listening. Even cooking took second place to hearing these tales. I finally stepped into the other room to better hear, as well as see if Mary had remembered to put fresh flowers on the table.

There sat my sister, prostrate near the teacher, transfixed like a lioness hungry for her food, never having given one thought to what I'd asked her to do! Nothing was done—no table set, no water put in a basin for their feet, and no oil was readied for their heads! Nothing! My nose flared like an enraged bull! Of all the times for her to . . . !

A whiff of scorched cake pulled me into consciousness and toward the oven. The raisin cakes—absolutely useless now!

Anger filled my chest. I smashed my foot down into the dirt, threw an iron skillet at the fire, and cursed loudly. Of all nights to burn the cake! I wanted this to be perfect! And where was Mary?

I exploded into the dining room ready to pounce on my sister, but for some reason, my face fixed on our simply dressed guest. It then dawned on me—he was really the reason this disaster was happening! He didn't care that I was in the other room working myself into a dither, trying to be a good hostess, laying my life down to serve people I didn't even know. He didn't even have the courtesy to wait to tell his stories until I could hear them! He didn't seem to even notice that I was gone. It looked to me like he already preferred Mary to me, just like Father!

I couldn't hold it in anymore, and I indicted him like the Sadducees winning a point for the law: "Don't you care that my sister has left me to do all this work by myself? I need help! Tell her to get up and help me!"

The glowing warmth in the room just seconds before was punctured by the frost that spewed from my mouth. Even I shivered from the chill of it.

Jesus looked at me for a moment.

"Martha," he said. Then he paused. "Martha," he said once more.

He paused again, letting me bask in the genuine kindness of his tone. He continued looking at me almost with curiosity, yet his voice retained the most authentic gentility.

"You are worried and upset about so many things."

"I am not just upset; I'm furious! I need help, and look at this lazy sister of mine who—"

My jumbled thoughts seemed to slow down before I could speak them aloud. In an instant, I perceived he was speaking about something more important than a meal.

"You are worried…"

How did he know? I wondered. I didn't want to admit it then, but he was right.

For several weeks prior to that day, I had been experiencing a growing concern about what would happen if one of us became ill. None of us had ever married, and there was no spouse to share our fortune or care for us when we were sick. We had no children, and we were advancing in years. Who would look after Mary or Lazarus if something happened to me? The knots in my shoulders had grown into deeper spasms up and down my back. Internally and externally, I was aware that I was writhing in fear and stress. *What if something was wrong with me now?*

"You are worried and upset about so many things, but only one thing is needed," he said.

At that, Jesus' hand turned inward and half-pointed toward himself.

The muscles in my jaw tightened like a clenched fist. *How audacious that this young man would walk into my house and reverse my code of conduct by suggesting he was more important! The gall!*

Defiance rose in my cheeks as my body began to quake. *How dare someone this fresh, this brazen, challenge my authority in my own home!*

But then, just as determinedly, and with a dominion that completely overshadowed mine, he stated with simple but tender firmness: "Mary has chosen what is better, and it will not be taken away from her."

That unexpected rebuke stung my cheeks with a crimson flush.

Boiling resentment started to percolate deep in my stomach, but for some unexplainable reason, I did something unusual. I held my temper. I instantly recognized that I had a choice. I could huff off into my normal, wounded tizzy, nursing my exasperation, and play the martyr, or I could acknowledge that my need to provide, to be perfect, to maintain my image was not more important than coming to know this one that was sitting quietly, waiting to reveal himself in patient power to one so impatient with her own lack of power.

The room was quiet. The other men were sitting with their eyes to the floor, clearly uncomfortable. Mary looked at me, tears cascading down her cheeks. She looked back at Jesus and then at me. Trembling, she moved her skirt to the side to provide a place for me at his feet, holding out her hand to me in timid, joyful hope.

What was I to do now? I wiped my face and eyes with my apron, pretending it was perspiration. The food, the energy, the time—everything in me was on the line. My entire identity was now challenged before a room full of strangers and my family, not to mention him. How humiliating!

I looked at Jesus from the corner of my eye. He was simply waiting.

It was in that instant, for an inexplicable reason, I suddenly and simply believed him. And not only that, I also believed *in* him. The essence of everything he said was rooted in an indefinable, intangible love. No one had ever spoken like that to me before. I was confronted with the recognition that my need to accomplish, my compulsion to be perfect, my fear of losing control were necessarily challenged in order to embrace a more important mission—absorbing the presence of the Holy One, from whom all accomplishment was to have its meaning.

I let out a long, last, deep sigh, my frame sinking to the floor beside my sister. For the first time in years, Mary and I fell into each other's arms and cried.

Lazarus, his cheeks wet with joy, put his hand to my face and whispered in my ear, "We need you."

A stubborn dam of resistance broke within me, and as it did, I felt able to walk into a new life-giving stream, a stream of knowing and being known, holding hands with my sister, my brother, and my new-found Lord.

Suddenly, I was aware in the pit of my stomach that I was famished, famished for the meat of this Lamb. It all became clear. The delicacies of this table far outweighed my own. Little did I know that we would enjoy dessert before dinner that night, and that raisin cakes would hold little appeal to the sweetness formed by every word of his mouth.

I had not only invited into my home and heart a teacher, but now a friend—one who loved me right where I was, and called me to where I needed to be—free to just be.

REFLECTIONS

"Free To Just Be"

1. Like Martha's back, what are the "spasms" in your life? (What stress do you carry and where?)

2. If you're a "Martha," what's your story? What belief systems do you carry about responsibilities?

3. Did your father not give you the affirmation you needed, so you try to get it through performance?

4. How does responsibility overrule your time for relationships?

5. With whom would you like to develop more relationship?

6. What can you do to enjoy life more fully?

7. Are there any ways that you "play the martyr?"

8. Do you manage to stay busy and avoid time with the Master?

9. Do you blame Jesus (or others) for things or events that interrupt your perfectionism or your agenda?

10. Have you categorized yourself as someone more mature, who doesn't need the time and affirmation of your Father as much as the younger ones?

11. Does God seem to ignore your need to be included?

12. Do you feel like you're always on the outside looking in, never in the thick of things? (Who put you on the outside?)

13. Are you safer in the kitchen? What are the pots and pans you're hiding behind?

14. If Jesus is just a step away, what are you getting by staying in the kitchen?

15. What is it about the "Marys" in life that irritates you?

16. Do you give yourself a badge of honor by "laying your life down?"

17. Are you always looking for people to validate you for your hard work, self-sacrifice, or creative caretaking?

18. Has anybody ever really seen or heard your heart?

19. What's keeping you from sharing it?

20. What's your secret fear?

21. Like Martha, what are the things you're worried and upset about?

22. Why are you afraid to be a Mary?

23. Do you feel Martha gets disrespected too much?

"Martha. Martha." Feel the kindness of his voice. He adores Martha! "Jesus loved Martha and her sister . . ." (John 11:5). He loves her creativity, her servant's heart. He delights in her hunger to please, to sacrifice, and to use her organizational skills. He just longs for time to be with her (and you). He wants to re-parent her and address the lies she's grown up with:

"Everyone else is more important."
"I get my worth from my job."
"My value lies in being a mother or a wife or . . . ?"
"I'm past my prime."
"My pain doesn't matter."
"I've got to hold onto control or everything will fall apart."

24. Jesus entered Martha's turf, challenging her authority. What turf are you trying to protect?

Jesus didn't confront Martha directly. He just showed her a higher way in contrast. He wasn't going to deprive the hungry-hearted by catering to the hungrily controlling. (Are you willing for your life to be used as a contrast to someone else's, and do it without apology or without lowering the standards he's called you to?)

25. When God loves you enough to show you a different, higher way, are you going to turn away in a huff and maintain your lonely isolation?

Dear one, the rest of the family is enjoying His presence. They're telling stories of real miracles, being amazed at the power of love. Are you parked where the air is humid with pretend responsibilities . . . "making sandwiches Jesus didn't ask for?" (Bill Johnson).

"Martha. Martha. "You're worried and upset about so

many things, but only one thing is needed." Your sisters have moved their skirts to the side. Will you sink to the floor and let your dignity go? Will you let them enfold you with their joyful tears and sit at his feet together?

Will you let the Lord change your appetites and redirect them toward true delicacies that will fill your heart that is starving for affection?

Let your hunger out. Come and dine. Open your mouth and feast on the one meal you need—the Lamb of God.

Receive his permission to just be.

Chapter Five

HE WILL COME

John 11:1-16

Jesus and his friends had come to dinner (and breakfast and noon meals) at our house many times since that first memorable night. Although old habits take time to die, I recognized a shift in my thinking that began to temper my compulsive caretaking. I found an inner permission to sit and enjoy my guests rather than just serve them. I started seeking out my neighbors and enjoying tidbits of time with them instead of making my tasks the priorities of my day.

I also realized there had been a new beginning in my relationship with Mary and Lazarus. Instead of cleaning up after a meal, we would linger, sometimes for an hour or more, discussing, wondering out loud, debating about what the Master had said or done that changed our way of understanding God.

After Jesus' repeated visits, I recognized that I was able to laugh more readily and heartily, as if the pall of adulthood had broken, and I was once again transported into the sweet childlikeness that I missed from long ago. Lazarus had even commented that a new color had come into my face.

Unfortunately, most of the color had recently gone out of his. For several weeks I noticed there had been an increasing pallor to his skin tone. He had begun to look sallow, like the color of the saffron dust we used to paint on our faces when we were children, hiding beneath the spice seller's table.

I arose late that morning, tired from thinking through the preparations for the upcoming Passover. I ate the last of the soft cheese our neighbor had brought for us on his business trip to Greece. Mary had been up for a long while and was already out enjoying herself, dispensing figs and dates and persimmons to travelers on the road to Jerusalem.

Uncharacteristically, Lazarus had gone to bed early for several nights in a row. I presumed he was now outside feeding the animals, but something made me walk toward his room.

The closed curtain in his doorway made my heart beat a little faster. I hesitated speaking to him, partly because if he were there, I didn't want to wake him, and partly because I wanted to believe he was simply working outside.

It was when I decided to walk away that I heard him moan.

"Brother? Lazarus?" I asked apprehensively.

When I pushed the curtain aside and looked at him, I physically shuddered. His lean, tall frame was shaking as if he were freezing, but he was soaked in sweat. The whites of his eyes were dark mustard yellow. Almost overnight his skin had turned a sickly golden-green. He was breathing heavily through his mouth, and I could see his tongue was chalky white.

He didn't seem to be able to move. His eyes said it all. From the panicked look on his face, I knew that the same illness, which had consumed our father, was now chewing on every corner of his being like a devouring, mocking hyena.

"Martha, I'm so tired. I can't move. And … and look," he said dejectedly, with tremendous effort.

Trying not to visibly shake, I walked over and saw that he had soiled his bed.

"All of a sudden, in the night." He shut his eyes in humiliation.

"Shhh." I comforted him, wiping his face with my apron. "Don't worry. I'll take care of it."

I tried to gather my racing thoughts. *Not Lazarus. No. Not Lazarus, too.*

"You're going to be fine. It must have been Mary's cooking last night." We both tried to laugh, but it didn't help.

He reached for my arm with terror in his eyes.

"Just like Father, Martha," he said. "Just like Father."

He lifted his arms to show me his skin tone, choking back the tears welling in his jaundiced eyes.

His voice had a hollow, tubular sound that burrowed into the depths of my soul like the voice of a man from a foreign country. I had to steady myself to look at him a second time. This voice, this body, was not my brother. The auburn-colored hair, high cheekbones, dark round eyes—they were all there. But my brother—my rock—was slipping away from me like a mudslide after a heavy rain.

I cleared my throat to call up that peaceful tone I use when I want everyone to stay calm, especially me. But my words sounded shallow, like my breathing.

"Lazarus, you're going to be all right. I'm going to get the physician. I'll be right back," I told him. "Just rest. I'm just going into…"

As I left his room I broke into a cold sweat and leaned against the wall, feeling as if I might vomit. This couldn't be happening. *Oh, dear Jehovah! He looked so sick!* I heard Mary enter the kitchen from outside. I had to intercept her before she came down the hall.

I steadied myself and staggered into the kitchen. Mary stopped singing when she saw how pale I was and rushed over.

"Sister, are you...?"

The clamminess of my skin caught her attention, and she sat me down quickly and drew some water.

"Do you have the fever? What's wrong? Your face is..."

She darted around the kitchen just as I would have, hoping to find something to make me feel better. Suddenly I saw a picture of myself, hurrying around and trying to help, when all I really wanted was for her to sit with me, just as she had done with Jesus. Almost instinctively, she put down the wet rag and knelt down, comforting me with her cool hands. I wanted to fall apart in her arms. She appeared so much stronger than I.

"Lazarus," I gasped. "I think—"

The terror of what I most feared must have sent an anguished look across my face because she instantly recoiled from me, as if she'd been electrocuted by an unseen shock.

"What's wrong? Where is he?"

"Lazarus? Where are you?" she called as she tore quickly down the hall and into his room. From where I was I could hear her inhaling. Waiting for what I thought would be hysterics, Mary's voice dropped to a tone I'd never heard coming from her before. With a sober, dynamic authority, she simply but firmly stated, "We're sending for the Master."

Yes, yes, not the physician, the Master! Thank God, someone could think clearly. Someone else could take charge, I thought. I felt so relieved that I cried.

When Mary returned to the kitchen, it was clear her voice was the only thing that had remained calm. She collapsed next to me, shaken and pale. We clung to each other, trying to keep our sobs as hidden as possible from Lazarus' ears.

"He looks like—" she whispered.

"Yes, I know," I interrupted, wiping my nose. "Did you see his hands twitching?" She nodded, closing her eyes.

"Martha...what if he...like Father?" She fell into me and muffled her weeping with her shawl.

"We must find Jesus right away," I said.

"Yes, Jesus. We must find Jesus."

We hugged each other and comforted ourselves with the words, "He will come. He will come."

That thought strengthened me enough to run out the door and down the street.

Jesus had told us he was going to the villages beyond the Jordan to preach, but we didn't know where. Our neighbor had a son, Boaz, who had recently celebrated his bar mitzvah. When I explained our desperate need, his father gave him permission to go and search for the Master. A new sense of heroism arose in the boy. There was no question he would accomplish his mission. Relying on all the resoluteness his 13-year-old frame could muster, I sent him off with explicit instructions: "Say to Jesus, 'The one you love is sick.'"

Boaz, whose name means swiftness (I prayed his father named him aright), alighted on his father's donkey with confidence. The animal brayed, and his ears went back as if a stubborn, mighty wind was blowing against him. But just as stubbornly, Boaz pressed the beast on, making immediate headway with the urgency we had hoped he would have. He waved a gallant goodbye as he crested the hill and rode away.

"He will not fail," his father encouraged me. I nodded my thanks, grateful to God for such a community, and I ran to tell Mary and Lazarus.

"If all goes well, he could be back day after tomorrow, maybe even tomorrow night!" I exclaimed.

That thought lightened all our fears. Even Lazarus was able to sit up and talk...until his body began to discharge the broth I was able to feed him.

All that day and night, Lazarus fought with every breath to

reject the creeping malignancy that made his muscles begin to twitch, his legs jerk, and his inner parts fail. He didn't have the energy to speak, and yet volumes poured through his eyes to each of us, saying perhaps more than he had said in all his life.

Mary and I would talk to him of pleasant things, mostly good memories, reminding him of how he was loved, how we needed him, and that Jesus would soon be here. With each comment about the Lord, his spirit seemed to rise, and his body would work to pull himself up a little higher in his bed. Whenever he was sleeping, his eyes would flutter as if straining to fight a heavy foreign hand from keeping them closed. He was in so much pain he would often yelp like a puppy that had lost its mother.

More than once, Mary and I would turn away and weep.

How could this be happening? I wondered. If anyone were to die, I thought that it would be me. I was the oldest.

That day and the next came and went as if they were one long night. The light hurt his eyes, so we darkened the room as much as possible and set candles nearby so he could see our faces. Mary and I continually peered out the window, hoping for a glimpse of a black-haired boy atop a donkey, along with the unforgettable figure of our friend and Lord, his arms encircling Boaz from behind.

Finally, about the twelfth hour of the second day, I walked toward the front door for some air. Neighbors had brought fresh fish and apples, olives and bread for supper. Grateful as I was, I was hungry for just one thing—Jesus' presence.

It was just after dusk, and the chill in the air was already cold. I saw Lazarus' prayer shawl sitting next to the oil lamp, and I could visualize him, as the man of the house, praying three times a day at that place on the floor, as was his custom. I picked up the small leather boxes containing bits of scripture, the Tefillin, as well as Lazarus' skullcap. I made a mental note to give these to Jesus when he came.

It was just then we heard the commotion. Boaz had returned! I rushed outside calling to Mary, breathless to lay my eyes on the Master. The young man was wiping his face, drinking from a ladle his father held for him. Despite the cold, his face was still flushed from the hard ride.

"I rode all night . . . and I found him this morning," Boaz spurted out, eagerly trying to gulp some water. "He was in Perea. Some merchants told me where to go."

"Perea." I surveyed the faces, not seeing Jesus. "Yes. Where is he?" I demanded.

The boy stiffened, then spoke as if he had repeated it to himself over and over again.

"Jesus said, 'This sickness will not end in death. No, it is for God's glory, so that God's Son may be glorified through it.'"

He finished his recitation with a sense of accomplishment. But instead of complimenting him, I pulled him up by the shirt into my face, feeling half-crazed.

"Then where is he? Why didn't he come?"

"I don't know," Boaz quivered. "I told him just what you said—'Lord, the one you love is sick'—and he told me what I just told you, and then he went on teaching. He didn't get up or say anything else. I was worried he hadn't heard me. I even interrupted him to ask again if he were coming. He smiled at me and just repeated what he said: 'This sickness will not end in death. It is for God's glory, so that God's Son may be glorified through it.' Then he nodded his head, as if to send me off, and turned around to speak to those who were there."

My heart felt like it had been sawed in two. We were his friends! Weren't friends entitled to more consideration than this?

"That's all?" I interrogated. "Did he say anything else? Anything to Mary or me?"

"No. Nothing." The boy shivered in fear of what that meant.

I felt energy drain from my body like water from a hole in the bottom of a pot. Jesus wasn't coming! Our friend, our teacher, the one we believed to be the Christ, didn't care. He had chosen others over us...his friends.

Our neighbor held my arm since I must have staggered. He wasn't coming. *What were we going to do? How was I going to tell Mary?* The tears gushed like a torrent down my face. Everything I'd put my trust in was shattered. There must be some explanation. And what of Mary? She was even closer to the Master. I knew I had to hold my tears before she saw me.

But it was too late.

No sooner had Boaz finished speaking than I saw Mary's shoulders fly back like the wings of a broken bird. Her body fell back against a doorpost as she slid down to the floor. Her mouth gaped open a little like Lazarus' did these days when he was gasping for breath. Having cloaked herself from the cold in Lazarus' prayer shawl, Mary pulled the edges tighter around her shoulders, as if to blanket herself from the truth of what she had just heard, and stared blankly into the dust.

Again, I thought, there had to be some explanation. And then it struck me.

"Mary...maybe he can't come." I wiped my eyes. "Maybe it's too dangerous for him to come. The Jews tried to kill him when he was in Jerusalem. They know he comes here and stays. Our house is near the Mount of Olives. Many know he goes there to pray. It's possible they're spying on us even now!" I looked around with fear at the hillside looming over us.

"He isn't coming," Mary said numbly.

My head was swirling. This was not like the one we knew who was so alive with love that all he had to do was look in our direction for us to feel his affection.

"Maybe he didn't know Lazarus is so sick," I volunteered. "Maybe all this was my fault! I must not have said it in just the right way. Maybe he's not responding because I didn't do it right!"

Venomous voices of accusation flooded my thoughts.

"God did not hear our prayers," Mary mumbled softly as if she couldn't believe her own words.

Just then, Lazarus screamed so fiercely from his room it was as if a cat-o'-nine-tails was scourging him from deep within. Mary and I jumped to our feet and ran toward the house.

When we crossed the threshold of his room, his yellowed, quivering hand was pointing to the hardened mud ceiling. His eyes were heavenward, as if seeing a place of radiating glory. His face appeared youthful. Although it was still slurred, his stammering speech resonated with strength he'd not had in several days.

"I see him!" Lazarus beamed.

For an instant I wanted to look where he was looking, as if Jesus might be surprising us by coming through the roof. I dared not take my eyes off Lazarus. His eyes filled with tears of euphoric joy, widening with glee, and his cheeks were lifted into the same radiant smile that he had the day he first met the Master. He looked so alive! His eyes shifted to me, and then to Mary, and in that instant, we both seemed to be pierced by the same inexpressible joy that burrowed deep into our souls.

As his face returned to gaze upward, Lazarus' head suddenly slumped back, landing sideways on the feather-filled cushion beneath him. With an uncontrollable lurch, his eyes turned inward and upward. A long, unusual sigh escaped his gaping mouth, and then the life instantly and completely drained away from his face.

He had departed.

I half-screamed, thinking he had a seizure. Mary held his face, speaking his name over and over. We tried to rouse him by telling him that Jesus was on his way. But there was no more breath, no more life.

Mary and I looked at each other, stunned with disbelief.

Lazarus was dead.

I remember little of the next several days. The Chevra Kadisha, a group of Jewish elders who prepare people for burial, came and washed his body as they recited prayers, observing the laws of our forefathers. His torso, arms, and legs were anointed with perfume. They bound his hands and feet, along with his jaw, to keep those parts from flailing open when the stiffness set in. Two of them dressed his body in linen shrouds, placing shaved pieces of pottery on his eyes and mouth, before the group carried him in procession to our family tomb outside Bethany.

When they rolled the stone in front of the tomb, it was as though they rolled a stone in front of Mary's heart. She collapsed into a pit of sorrow deeper than she could bear.

The Meal of Consolation, served to mourners by their neighbors after a burial, did nothing to lift the desolation from my soul. Lazarus had left me. And now, unbearably, it appeared that Jesus had as well, since it had been four days since we had placed our brother in the grave. Four days! Mary had refused to come out of her room, ignoring pleas to visit with relatives, and even scandalously refusing to give up Lazarus' prayer shawl when the elders asked to wrap it around his shoulders before burial. She didn't care that, as a woman, wearing the *tallit* was forbidden. It was an unusual act of defiance . . . similar to her sitting at the feet of Jesus.

For four days she had enfolded herself in Lazarus' shawl like a caterpillar in a cocoon. And for five days, we waited, but no change came.

Jesus' words, "This sickness will not end in death," felt like a promise as cold as our brother's body. Everyone knew that bodies begin to decay on the third day. How could life spring from a decaying corpse?

The evidence was mounting that Jesus might be a charlatan. But in my heart, I couldn't bear the thought. It was too much. That grief was so great that it was almost as hard to take as the loss of my brother. Now, not only was my Lazarus gone, but so was my Messiah, the one who brought new life and freedom to me. Could he really have disregarded our pleas and allowed our brother to die? Did he not care to bring us any comfort in our sorrow?

Four days after he died, utterly exhausted, I asked the friends who came to grieve with us one morning during *shiva* to leave me alone for a while.

I stood alone in the room where we had invited Jesus and his men for their first meal in our home. There was the table where we had served the lamb, the place where they all had reclined. I positioned myself on the spot where Jesus apprehended me about my drivenness, and closed my eyes tightly to recall his words: "You are worried and upset about so many things, but only one thing is needed." That was when Jesus had pointed to himself.

I paced around the room in a physical and emotional frenzy, aching with disillusionment. Muscle spasms were tightening their grip throughout my body. My heart felt raw with confusion and anguish. The ancient Psalm ran through my mind: "The cords of death assail me..."

In an eruption of buried grief, a raspy accusation flew from my throat: "How can I trust that you're the one thing I need when you let something like this happen? You said, 'This sickness will not end in death.' You lied to me! You betrayed our friendship! You've left me all alone!"

I collapsed to the floor, and with all the remaining strength I had, limply pulled at the customary Jewish tear in my clothing once again—a piece of fabric, once united, now torn into two pieces.

I looked more closely at it. It was still the same cloth, only separated. Something had caused division, but I stopped to think: *Was it Jesus who did the separating, or was it I?*

I was startled back to reality with a heavy banging on the front door.

Boaz was breathing rapidly, having run across the way. "He's come!" he exclaimed. "The Master has come to Bethany!"

I ran outside to look. Right at the crest of the hill at the edge of the city was the outline of the young carpenter and his band of brothers walking stalwartly in the mid-morning sun.

Before I could defend against it, a rush of hope burst into my chest and down my legs, catapulting my feet toward Jesus. I felt a little bit out of my mind, laughing and weeping at the same time. All that mattered was that he had come, and I was no longer alone.

As I ran through the maze of homes in the village, I lost sight of where he was. A grievous moan from the pit of my stomach stretched into an inner scream.

"Don't leave me again!"

I ran and ran, then turned around a corner and lost my footing on some sand, scraping my knee. When I looked up, Jesus was on the path, holding my gaze. He was blinking hard and rapidly, and his chest seemed to move in and out like Lazarus' when he died. But he didn't move.

Jesus waited for me to get up and move toward him.

I felt the unbearable swirl of my heartache within me swirl like a giant vortex of angry wind. I careened toward him, falling right in front of him, when he caught my arms and pulled me to his face.

The thunder in my voice rose steadily, and before I could think, I angrily assaulted him: "If you had been here, my brother would not have died!"

My words slapped his face worse than my hand ever could. Something in me wanted to hurt him, to shake him, but just at that second, the same vigorous hope that leapt within me when I saw him crest the hill poured out of my mouth with a statement that startled even me:

"But I know that, even now, God will give you whatever you ask."

What? Lazarus was dead. Why did I say this?

His swift, dark eyes looked at me with an unexpected eagerness.

"Your brother will rise again," he declared.

All of our after-meal conversations came flowing back to my thinking.

"I know he will rise again in the resurrection at the last day," I said almost mechanically, still not understanding our strange verbal dance.

His tone and pacing increased: "I am the resurrection and the life. He who believes in me will live, even though he dies; and whoever lives and believes in me will never die. Do you believe this?"

The fire of faith within him began to ignite in me, and something in me rose into an expectation I could not express. It began burning out the accusations, the sense of betrayal, and the despondency over his not coming.

"Yes, Lord!" I almost shouted.

With those words, a strange power moved from my mouth down into the rest of my being. For the first time in the history of our relationship, I practically screamed, without shame, the naked truth of what was in my heart:

"I believe! I believe you are the Christ, the Son of God, who was to come into the world!"

His breathing on my face was so powerful it seemed to enter my nostrils and march into my mind, disbanding the army of angry, accusing thoughts. Within seconds I saw him for who he was—the living Messiah—and I knew nothing was impossible.

And like Andrew, who first met Jesus and ran to get his brother, Peter, I too had to run and get my sister.

REFLECTIONS

"He Will Come"

Martha had moved from martyr to truster. She had grown in her relationship with Christ and had become his friend more than his servant. How Jesus must have loved the new relationship he enjoyed with her! He must have enjoyed the relationship he had with the entire family.

It was in the security and trust of that relationship that the Father designed a "bigger story."

Lazarus was not only Mary and Martha's only brother but probably their breadwinner. He was the male voice of authority, perhaps the voice of reason in their home, and their masculine anchor. To have him struck with a terminal illness and unexpectedly die would have rocked their world.

It challenged:

- their security, financially and emotionally,
- their trust in Jesus' words, and
- their belief in God's goodness.

The fact is, they were *blindsided*.

1. What do you think is the difference between expectation and hope? (One answer is that expectation "demands," and hope "asks.")

2. Have you expected God to perform as you've demanded?

3. When he hasn't come according to your timetable or in the way you anticipated, have you turned your back on him to punish him?

4. Do you feel like he's your friend, and that friends are entitled to greater consideration?

5. Have you ever thought: "I must not have prayed right. I
didn't say it right, so he didn't answer," and you go into a
tirade of accusing thoughts against yourself?

6. When something bad happens now, do you filter your
thinking through the lens of "If God is good, how could he
have let this happen?"

In this version, Martha actually proves her character. She
tells Jesus the truth of what was in her heart. She is authentic
in her grief with him—pouring out her feelings and dis-
charging the toxins in her emotions. Then like David, she still
chooses to believe in Him.

Is it possible that telling the truth may have gotten her
ready to move from unbelief to belief?

7. The Scripture doesn't record that Jesus asked to see Mary.
Did Martha build a bridge between Jesus and Mary? Did she
hear the heart of God for her sister and become his mouth-
piece of reconciliation and healing?

The statement, "He will come," is a comment of trust in
their Lord's love. "He will come" was a remark of security
about their friendship. "He will come" also became an expectation of entitlement. Mary and Martha expected Jesus to come
and rescue them from their need and do it in their timetable.

My friends, we see through this passage that indicting or
accusing God is arrogance and is something of which we must
repent. It gives entrance to the enemy to torment us. We need
to renounce any agreement with a spirit of arrogance, and repent of any accusation against God of wrongdoing. We need to
take authority over those strongholds and command them to

leave in the name and power of Christ, asking him to fill us with his Holy Spirit of humility and trust, knowing "he does all things well."

Chapter Six

TAKING AWAY THE STONE

John 11:17-44

The pain of losing my brother was so severe, I felt like my skin had been seared with hot oil. I was so tender I thought that if anyone came close enough to breathe on me, even Martha, I felt like I, too, might die.

An interior death mask had been placed over my heart, and I was molding myself into position to wear it the rest of my life. Could there even be life without Lazarus? My effervescent, lifeline of a brother was gone—the one male I thought I could depend on. *Another* man had abandoned me. First Father did, then Lazarus, and now this God-man, this Jesus of Nazareth, whom I had instantly loved with every song in my soul, had ignored and rejected me, preferring strangers over me during my most desperate need.

I inhaled quickly to avoid more tears. Thinking of him being just down the road, waiting for Martha to come, made me turn over and pull Lazarus' prayer shawl even tighter around my shoulders.

He's not trustworthy, a voice inside said. *He didn't come when you needed him. Don't humiliate yourself by going to him. What good would that do? Lazarus is dead.*

I had been to a doctor once where I was given a potion to drink to make my head stop hurting. In a few minutes, a creeping dullness, a strange, drunken disconnection between my mind and my body occurred, and I didn't feel anything. I just existed.

That was how I was feeling when Martha stormed into my doorway.

Disregarding the curtain, I opened my eyes in time to see her get down on her knees beside me. With a swollen, sweaty hand on my face she blurted excitedly: "The teacher is here and is asking for you."

Her voice didn't sound normal for someone in mourning. It was higher pitched, excited, and hopeful.

"What?" I mumbled.

"He's here. He wants to see you."

"Why? He ignored our call. Why should I hear his?" I jerked my face away from her touch.

Martha looked at me as if she didn't know me. I could see the blood drain out of her face as her hand slid away. The shock of it startled even me.

"I'm sorry, Martha, I—"

I started to get up. That dazed stupor I had been in for so long began to dissipate as I did. I felt like I was coming out of a coma. *Where was I? Where had I gone?*

Being so weak, I started to fumble for my clothes, but then had to lie down again. It must have heartened Martha because she picked me up under my arms and helped me stand. I was still dizzy. My speech was slurred a little, like I had been awakened out of a deep sleep.

"Jesus? Where is he?"

"Just outside the village, where the road turns to Jericho. Here are your shoes. Let me help you."

Martha poured a cup of water for me and quickly began to brush my hair. The water seemed to help both my body and my mind. With each tug from the brush on my head, my head snapped back into a clearer sense of reality. Jesus had come. He had always been life to me, and he was here now.

The contrast in my thinking between then and a moment before surprised me. I felt alert now as though Martha had pulled me out of my own grave. In losing Lazarus, death had somehow taken on a life of its own. Life had become all about loss, pain, hopelessness, and betrayal, not about joy, love, hope or the future. The dank, musty coldness in my mind was brightened by one thought—my Messiah had asked for me!

Would I not come?

Suddenly, I had no time for details. Comfort had come! Martha still had my brush in her hand when I bounded out the door. She wasn't far behind.

The road to Jesus that day seemed unforgiving and long. As quickly as I had begun to run toward him, dark, accusing thoughts began to re-emerge: *If you had been Jesus today, you would have rushed to your home, enveloped you in an embrace, and wept with you in the hour of your greatest desolation. But he is requiring that in your physical weakness and emotional exhaustion you have to get up off your bed and run out to see him! How fair is that?*

For a moment, all that began to make sense. Something in me began to agree, but in the agreement, I felt the life-sucking tentacles of that familiar stupor begin to invade my energy and my joy. I shook myself for even considering those thoughts. I would use my feet to demonstrate who I would spend my time listening to, thank you very much! *Out of my way!*

I must have looked like quite a sight because everyone in

town stopped and watched me run down the street. The farther I got, the more I realized his wisdom in not coming to me. His beckoning had broken my isolation, my self-protection. He knew that if I wanted him, I had to be forced to come out of hiding. I had to stop nursing my hurt.

Still, I indulged myself a little. I leaned over to Martha who had caught up with me by this time and said, "Why did our house have to be on the opposite end of the town? Couldn't he at least come through a little closer to our side?"

Martha laughed out loud, and despite my self-pity, I did a little, too. It felt good.

A young boy darted in front of my path and out of the way. My mind flashed back to when I first saw Jesus as he healed that boy near our home. It was the day we first met. When he first looked at me, I got lost in his eyes. This strong, strapping carpenter had a magnetism of such compelling, but tender, power that everything in me wanted to know him. I had never known those qualities in a man.

I ran past a woman dressing a quail for the noon meal. The scene when Jesus kindly rebuked Martha for demanding my help with dinner cascaded through my mind. Here was someone who didn't expect anything from me! A tidal wave of joy had enveloped me that night. Here was a man who gave me permission to be just who I was, who indulged my thirst for knowledge and intimacy and contemplation, all without reprimand. Here was someone who simply enjoyed me!

Although I secretly adored him, I suspected he knew that. But he loved us, all the women, in a paradoxical way; near, yet far; intimately, but with a kind of restrained abandonment. He was not unlike Lazarus, who loved me as a sister, but also as a friend. It was because of that trustworthiness that, when we called him about Lazarus and he didn't come, I felt I had lost not one brother but two.

As I approached the last of the town's streets, I was suddenly aware of the dozens of family and friends who were running with me. Were they running to comfort me, or did they want to see him too? Those who had stayed in town earlier appeared to have joined our ranks with every turn. By the time Martha and I arrived, most of the village had run ahead and surrounded him, for they had heard of this man's power.

There was an unusual quiet that permeated this crowd. On the occasions when Jesus had visited before, the miracles he did created crackling cheers throughout the group, with waves and waves of outstretched hands worshipping and praising the living God. But this time, an energy that could not be described seemed to muffle any physical expression.

As I made my way up the street, people around him parted so that we could meet. He was standing in the center of the crowd, taller than I had ever seen him. It was when I saw his face that I again realized my weakness and the reality of my fractured heart.

I tried to call out to him but it was as though my throat had tightened closed. His outstretched arms seemed to transmit an enabling strength to my trembling legs.

Just one more step, I told myself. *One more step.*

When I finally collapsed at his feet, I felt like I had shattered into tiny splintered fragments, unable any longer to hold myself together. All I could do was pant.

Instantly, I felt his large, warm hand reach down and stroke my head. The tenderness and strength of it was like a lever releasing the pool of grief within my soul. I could hold it inside me no longer.

"Lord, if you had been here, my brother would not have died!" I screamed.

My broken heart must have touched a communal nerve. The uproar of weeping that rose from the crowd seemed to blend like an unrehearsed chorus, each one expressing their personal loss. Everyone had loved Lazarus. They had lost a counselor, a friend, a fair businessman. They would no longer experience his laughter, his wisdom, or his friendship. The community had buried one of its beloved, and they, too, were yet to be consoled.

I heard Jesus' breathing change into a strange, brooding sound, like a windy tempest brewing over the Dead Sea. His voice vibrated with a deeper, huskier tone.

"Where have you laid him?" he asked.

"Come and see," some men replied.

It was then I could feel the heat of his body as he bent over toward me on the ground. I looked up to see his dark brown hair falling over his reddened face, hiding it from everyone else's view but mine. It was contorted in agony, and he looked almost angry. I blinked long and hard, trying to get a better picture. His silent tears fell on my face—large, God-sized tears, steaming with grief, mingling with my own.

I wept more.

So did he.

That moment was like a tunnel that was created between the two of us, and for the first time I saw his pain over our loss—his pain of having to restrain himself from coming when we sent word, his pain at knowing we would feel abandoned. Despite the pain, he chose to trust and obey his Father that this would be for God's glory. His pain was as real as ours.

At last I felt his heart. He understood.

And so did I.

He locked his eyes with mine and then closed his in a long, sustained clasp, as if it were an embrace his arms couldn't give.

We were friends again.

He stood up straight and brushed his eyes with the sleeves of his robe as Andrew helped me to my feet. The whole crowd watched intently as an inner fury filled his face. With resolute determination, he looked up and began walking—not toward our house, but toward the tomb!

Martha and I glanced at each other, almost unable to breathe. His message, "This sickness will not end in death," rushed to my lips, and I began to repeat it over and over like a prayer.

The moment he started toward the tomb, the community was electrified with anticipation, never having seen Jesus in this condition before. As each of us walked toward Lazarus' place of death, I wondered if any of us had ever felt more alive.

The closer we neared the tomb, the air took on a different quality. The dankness reminded me of the thoughts that had been swirling around in my head earlier that day. The sweet scent that seemed to be surrounding him and his band of believers appeared to neutralize whatever was foul there in the air.

In our culture, whenever we approached a tomb, we would be respectful, quiet, and careful. Jesus broke every rule. His gait didn't slow down—the closer he got, the faster it increased. With each step, an interior energy, a sense of command summoned him into a position of authority that far surpassed the centurions that rode our way. It was as if he were about to confront the Angel of Death and assail him for doing his job!

When we arrived at the tomb, there was a hand-hewn stone at the entrance, about the height of a grown man. Jesus' body language toward the stone looked almost confrontive. His face began to boil with angry indignation.

Martha and I looked at each other nervously. *What was he going to do?*

Some of the Pharisees from our village had filtered into the crowd, eyeing him with an obvious snarl of mistrust. I overheard one of them sneer, "Could not he who opened the eyes of a blind man have kept this man from dying?" His question faded into a jagged, jaded smile.

Jesus stared defiantly at him, then defiantly at the tomb. "Take away the stone!" he commanded.

I gasped along with the rest of the crowd.

Martha shook her head vigorously, pleading with him. "But Lord, by this time there is a bad odor! He's been in there four days!"

Jesus looked at her with ardent determination. "Did I not tell you that if you believed you would see the glory of God?"

To this, no one replied, not even Martha. For a moment, no one knew what to do. Then young Boaz, heroic Boaz, strode over to the stone and began to push against it with all his might. His father, surprised but proud, began to push alongside him. Others pushed and pulled, rocked and shoved, until the stone was dislodged and soon rolled to the side, laying bare the entrance to the tomb of our brother.

Martha and I began to weep. The Master had come after all!

Jesus looked up, his face to the sky. "Father, I thank you that you have heard me. I knew that you always hear me, but I said this for the benefit of the people standing here, that they may believe that you sent me."

Then, in a vehement, thunderous voice, Jesus commanded, "Lazarus, come out!"

A muted thumping sound began to emerge from the limestone tomb, like a heart beating deep within a dark chest cavity. The pounding lasted for more time than I could hold my breath.

My mind was racing, in turn, with hope, with terror, and with belief. Martha and I were on either side of the Master, breathless, waiting, our legs so weak we could barely stand.

The thumping continued, getting louder and louder. *What*

was happening? Only the dead lay in there! I saw a faint shadow, a movement of some kind. Was it my imagination? A scrap of white linen appeared in the entrance and then disappeared. But then, my brother, my Lazarus, still bound hand and foot, thumped out of the cave and into the morning sunlight! A shriek of such magnitude escaped my being that I had to lean on Jesus. The crowd screamed in amazement and wonder—hollering, weeping, dancing, and praising as they ran toward Lazarus.

"Take off his grave clothes and let him go!" Jesus commanded.

Some members of the Chevra Kadisha burial party, their hands shaking, tore off the face cloth that blocked his view, untied his jaw, and loosened his hands and his feet.

There was our brother, Lazarus, pink with health, bewildered but joy-filled, born again as a man without sickness!

As soon as he was free, Lazarus rushed over to where Jesus, Martha, and I stood rejoicing with laughter and tears. The three of us embraced Lazarus, still half-dressed in linen as if he were in swaddling clothes, like a child born in a manger not that long ago.

A piece of the white cloth flew away in the wind as if a shroud that had covered our community had been blown away by this man's breath of life. Truly, this sickness did not end in death. No, it was for God's glory!

Post Script from Martha:

I remembered when I had been standing in the room with Jesus several months before, he had said, "You are worried and upset about so many things, but only one thing is needed."

That night he had, in effect, raised me from the dead—the death of my self-preoccupations, my self-defenses, and my self-ishness. My mission *to do* was appropriately derailed in order that I could learn *to be*, and to experience a higher destiny of the Master for me than fulfilling my own agenda.

When Lazarus became sick, I was confronted yet again with my need to be in control—this time, my need to keep my brother alive. As horrifying as the prospect was to let go of, my plan was necessarily derailed by a different, more important mission—glorifying the Son of God, and letting him do whatever he might choose, however he might choose to do it, even if it were through my loss.

As it turned out, Lazarus' death and resurrection became the turning point for the Pharisees to begin the plot to kill Jesus. For without his own death, Jesus would not have become the Savior of the human race.

My point? It's not always about us.

In retrospect, when I looked at the whole picture—his delay, our sense of betrayal, Lazarus' death and returning to life, Jesus' death and resurrection—the thought occurred to me, *With whom else could he ever have trusted such an assignment, if not one of his friends?*"

REFLECTIONS

"Taking Away the Stone"

1. Have you experienced loss to the capacity that it seems to take on a life of its own? Life becomes about:
   Divorce
   The Empty Nest
   Finances
   Health
   Friendship
   Loss of a parent, child, spouse
   Loss of trust.

2. Have you ever felt like you're in a burn ward—so fragile you feel you'll die if anyone breathes on you?

3. Have you ever gone into a stupor where it's easier to not live than to feel the pain? (This is the slippery slope where the enemy invades us like bacteria to a wound and infects our thinking with lies.)

4. Are you there now?

5. What are the voices that have been, or are now going on?
   "God is not trustworthy."
   "He doesn't come when I need him."
   "I've got to take care of myself because no one else will."
   "My isolation is my drug of choice."
   "Staying in a stupor is easier than risking life."

6. Are you hiding in the bedroom of self-protection?

7. Are you willing to stop nursing hurt and come out into the light? Did you know he's willing to hear your questions such as,

"Why didn't he come sooner?
"Why didn't he answer when I called?"
"Where was he when I needed him?

Dear friend, his presence is waiting for you, even when he doesn't give you answers.

8. Are you willing to get off your mat, as Mary did, and take your first steps toward him? As you do, your strength will increase. As you do, you will be awakened from your stupor. As you do, you will be a magnet for people around you to come and know the Master. You may be the instrument he uses to draw your community to His side.

9. Are you willing to fall at his feet and let him weep with you over your loss? Are you willing to look up at his face and let his tears mingle with your own?

I want to encourage you to put away your desire to punish him. You are only depriving yourself of the comfort that you're most desperate for. He understands. His heart is toward you. His hand wants to release the lever of *your* grief and let a fresh stream of hope and life wash away your pain.

Not only that, he wants to resurrect your dreams. He wants to boldly march you toward the things you have thought had died—your marriage, health, relationships, ministry, self worth, even your purpose.

He wants to call you back into believing he is both a resurrector and a life-giver! "I am the resurrection and the Life!" (John 11:25)

And beyond that, Jesus calls you to be a part of a community. He wants you to be part of a group that will help take away the stone that has rolled across the entrance to your heart.

Taking away the stone, removing grave clothes, and releasing you is the work of the Body of Christ. The community is here to work together and leverage their efforts on your behalf. We are here to work shoulder to shoulder to remove the obstacles that are keeping you in the grave. No one can call himself out of the tomb. No one can remove his or her own grave clothes.

Many have problems with trust as a result of wounds previously received in the church. They know they're in grave clothes, entombed in loneliness and isolation, but they're terrified to come back into the community.

The Lord wants you to know he sees *you*. He knows the dark hole you live in. He hears the inner screams no one else is able to hear. He is saying, "Trust my ways. I'm calling you into the light, out of hiding. I will send you trustworthy helpers. Take the first step. Jump off your funeral pier and walk forward into the light by repenting of your judgments against my Body. When you reject my Body, you reject me, for I live in my Body. I long to embrace you through my Body, comforting, warming, and nurturing you back to life. I know the way. Trust me."

If you've made judgments against the Body of Christ, he longs to relieve that self-protective ache in you. Come to the Lord and repent of your wrong attitude toward pastors, leaders, friends, well-intentioned but ignorant churchgoers, legalists, or anyone who has rejected or slandered you. Let him fill you with his affection. Repentance will set you free.

Jesus' words, "This sickness (of mind, heart, body) will not end in death. No, it is for God's glory, that God's Son may be glorified through it" is a word for us today. When we repent, the sickness we've inflicted on ourselves through our judgments will cause what the enemy has intended for evil to be turned for good! God will be glorified!

God also glorified himself through Mary and Martha's suffering. Are you willing to let him do that, even if it is through your loss?

10. Are you willing to recognize that there is a story that is bigger than you? Can you let go of your need to understand?

11. Are you willing to trust that you are a player in the theater of the Kingdom, and he has trusted you with a role, however small, that is critical to the entire story?

12. Can you humble yourself from having to be "the star," around which everything else revolves, and be a bit player whose purpose is only to reflect him?

13. Can you ask for and receive the sweet humility that God wants to give you for your part?

14. Friend, have you been in a season of withdrawal, of being in a stupor from your injuries or sin or isolation, and you've bought into the lies about God that say: "He's not trustworthy," "He doesn't come when I need him," or "I'm still in the same place. What's the use?" Please get up from your bed now and walk toward him. He's waiting for you to choose life!

Chapter Seven

THE ANOINTING

John 12:1-9

I awoke in the middle of the night, my lungs heaving with fear. The morbid images from my nightmare kept spiraling in my thoughts. I could still see Lazarus' jaundiced, terrified eyes searching wildly for me; my prized alabaster full of spikenard perfume being pulled out of my hands to anoint Lazarus' body; Jesus' words clanging like gongs in my mind: "The Son of Man will be handed over to be crucified."

My forehead was beaded with sweat, and the thumping in my chest made me light-headed and nauseous. *Have I lost track of time? Was Lazarus still dead? Where was Jesus? Where was I?*

I stood up, trying not to shake. Collecting my thoughts, I managed to feel my way across the dark room to a bronze chest Father had given me as a child. *Was my alabaster vase still there, safely protected? Was this a dream, too?*

Fumbling with the clasp and trying not to awaken Martha, I opened the box. The moonlight suddenly broke through the clouds and was bright enough to highlight the luminescence of my milky-white marbled treasure. I let out a little joyful moan. It took all my energy to lift the heavy vial to my chest. I sat with it, cradling its coolness against the heat of my body.

"Thank you, God. Just a dream. No more loss. Only a dream."

But those terrifying words kept returning to haunt me: "The Son of Man must be delivered into the hands of sinful men, be crucified, and on the third day be raised again."

Those statements had been no dream. I'd heard Jesus say them myself.

I got up and pulled a shawl over my shoulders. "We've had enough death!" I whispered to no one. *Mother. Father. Lazarus. Now Jesus?*

"He always speaks in riddles," I mumbled to myself as I made my way down the stairs. I tried to adjust my thinking to a different time and space. This was reality, not my nightmare.

Still, he had said it, and I couldn't deny it, even though I wanted to. The statement pierced me through like a knife. *Was I the only one who heard those words? Was nobody else bothered by what he said?*

During those middle-of-the-night hours, my mind and I played a morbid game of hide and seek. It tormented me with what I most feared, and I held tightly onto the alabaster vial as measure of comfort, trying to rock myself to sleep. It was small consolation at that time of night, hard and uncomfortable. In the moonlight it took on the appearance of an enormous, un-worldly pearl. I recalled Jesus' parable about a man finding a large pearl buried in a field. He sold all that he had to buy the land so he could own that pearl of great price.

This was my pearl, I decided. When Father and Mother had died, their estate was divided three ways. Martha wanted the house. Lazarus wanted the business. And I wanted the alabaster jar and the perfume. Both my siblings offered to share their portions with me, but I didn't want them. I secretly believed I got the better deal because it brought such beauty, and it took no effort to maintain. I realized it was worth quite a lot, but that wasn't what mattered to me. What mattered was that it was precious.

Mother and I had always shared a love for fragrances, for beauty, and for, well, the impractical. My pearl may have been impractical to Martha and Lazarus. But just studying the sculpting of such a magnificent jar and inhaling the bouquet of the exotic, priceless oil called me to worship the God who would create such an astonishing scent from the root of an herb found in far-away India. It called me to adore the one who formed such magnificent alabaster from crystallized water drippings in some obscure underground cave.

As far as I was concerned, if anything would call me into greater worship of my God, I would say that that thing was very practical.

And yet, if I were honest with myself, there was even a greater pearl in my heart. Jesus' luster never seemed to fade. The container of his body held a fragrance more satisfying than any possession or inheritance I could know. And he had said that it must be broken, tortured, and crucified. Surely he was speaking in metaphors again. I had listened to him long enough to recognize the storyteller in him.

I finally made my way back to my room, tenderly putting away the jar, and prayed to God to help me go back to sleep. Mercifully, he did.

It was several days later when Simon, the local leper, greeted us with a broad smile and a sleeveless new tunic, proudly showing off his fresh, pink skin!

"Lazarus, look," he said. "Ten fingers, all there!"

They embraced and slapped shoulders. We had heard that Simon was one leper out of ten whom Jesus had healed and was the only one who had returned to thank him.

He and Lazarus instantly bonded—both crushed by the power of disease and death and both now restored to fullness of life through Jesus. That day our new companion had come to issue an invitation to a more formal act of appreciation—a banquet honoring Jesus for the healing he had given him. He asked all of us to join him in celebrating his healing and Lazarus' resurrection.

Lazarus immediately replied, "Yes, of course," but Martha and I stayed politely quiet.

I heard her whisper, "But Simon is a Samaritan!"

"That is not the trouble," I said as I pulled her away. "Jesus will be in danger."

The trouble was with the Pharisees.

Word had increasingly circulated that Jesus' appearances at the temple and in Jerusalem were considered to be dangerous by the chief priests. Many people had abandoned their former allegiances to the Jewish authorities and shifted them to Jesus, proclaiming him their king. Deeply threatened by this, the chief priests, we'd heard, had issued an order of arrest.

As Lazarus thanked Simon for the invitation, Martha and I hurried upstairs and went straight to prayer, afraid there might be trouble. It was then an extraordinary peace came over me, and my focus shifted. Suddenly I knew everything would be all right. I instantly realized no other occasion would be more worthy of opening the seal on my inheritance—my alabaster—than to celebrate the resurrected life of my brother by the Life-Giver.

It was the custom at some social engagements and feasts, like Simon's, for servants to enter the banquet carrying censers smoking with burning perfumes. Others, holding in their hands sprigs of sweet basil or some other plant, would dip them in perfumed water, and sprinkle them over the guests. Before dinner, the water in which they washed was also highly perfumed.[2] The anticipation of being the one carrying the perfumed censer, full of my spikenard oil, overwhelmed me. I only wished Mother had been there to enjoy it with me.

A few days before the Passover, Simon sent a cart to pick us up at our door. This small courtesy didn't escape any of us. I especially appreciated it since I had planned on carrying the heavy, concealed gift with me that evening.

Upon our arrival, Simon ushered us into the dining room. It was filled with several low-lying tables surrounded by goose-feather pillows of brightly colored fabrics from India and Egypt, favorites of Simon's. Our host seated Lazarus near the place of honor, right next to where Jesus would be.

Other guests had already arrived, and as Lazarus was seated, I noticed many of them started whispering and staring at my brother. Lazarus had always been content to be in the background in social settings. Although he had an inviting presence, he found himself most comfortable in the corner of a room sharing some intense thoughts with a friend or two around which there was always lively discussion.

For him to be front and center in a room of people he did not know was always a challenge. But adding to that, his overnight notoriety at being a man who was dead for four days was a double discomfort.

My anxiety increased for my brother as Simon's guests began asking questions of Lazarus, pressing him for details about his death and resurrection.

"What did you feel when your body began to die?" a large man with a silver bracelet boldly asked.

"Where did you go after you died?" queried a heavily be-jeweled woman.

"Were you conscious of anything in the tomb?" asked a young scribe.

"What happened to your body when Jesus called your name?" Simon's adolescent son queried excitedly.

I was half-angered by their relentless questions because Lazarus could barely take one in before another was asked. However, I understood their curiosity because Martha and I had asked the same things ourselves.

Lazarus told the same story publicly that he had told us privately. I noticed that every time he tried to talk about it, a kind of inner glory would envelope him from within and swallow up any consciousness about who he was in it all. It wasn't about him. It was about Jesus.

"To describe the experience is beyond me," Lazarus shared. "I'm simply the box, like the Ark of the Testimony in the time of Moses. Within me, God has chosen to keep memorials to his glory—his life-giving presence."

He tried to explain more, then just shook his head, overcome with humility, and quietly began to weep.

A gentle hush fell in the room, but it wasn't awkward or humiliating—it was reverent. His words had changed the atmosphere, setting the stage for even greater revelation to come.

I was about to speak to the guests and take the spotlight off Lazarus when Martha pulled me into the kitchen. I looked at her crossly, but her voice was sweet and endearing.

"I saw your alabaster. Will you let me help you? I noticed the herb garden as we rode up. You need basil sprigs. Wait right here." Martha hurried out to the garden before I could even answer her. Her eyes had held a misty pride in me. For a moment, I thought she would burst into tears, as she had been known to frequently do of late. I smiled and sighed, relieved that she knew what I was planning on doing and wasn't going to scold me.

The Anointing

I noticed a large carafe of olive oil and vinegar together in one bottle, but still separated. The practical and the impractical don't always mix, but somehow, sometimes, they do. And so it was that evening with me and my sister.

As I waited for Martha, I was amazed at the dinner preparations Simon had so lavishly readied. A full bullock had been strung, roasted, and carved, along with three pheasants, some quail, and a large garnished lamb. Wineskins hung from the rafters that criss-crossed in the kitchen, and loaves of whole grain yeast bread filled the air with their nutty fragrance. Sugar almonds garnished platters of plump pomegranates, sour green apples, dates the size of my big toe, and ripened figs—all ready for the guests to enjoy.

Martha hurried back in with a basket of basil and a carafe of water. "I saw Simon and explained, and he was honored to have you do this," she smiled. The sprigs were fresh and sweet, and as Martha handed them to me, she uncharacteristically kissed my face.

"From Mother," she said. And we both blinked hard.

It was then we heard the Lord arrive with his disciples. Upon his entrance, everyone's attention was suddenly riveted on him.

Simon could hardly contain himself.

"Come, Master! Welcome! Welcome to my home!"

Simon signaled for the music to begin. In an instant, the anticipation of the whole house seemed to rise in celebration of the one who is life and gives life.

Those who had never seen Jesus before were startled by his disheveled appearance as a result of his travel that day from Jerusalem. We heard some murmuring from his disciples about his dealing with some money changers at the temple. His hair was uncombed, his feet and hands were dirty, and he smelled of sour sweat. I instantly noticed a small cut bleeding on the top of his foot.

Simon parted the way between guests for Jesus to enter the room, but instead of moving forward, the Master paused for a minute and surveyed the faces of those who had been waiting for him. His eyes lingered on each guest, as if to savor everyone's personal presence. When they fell on Martha and me, I thought for a moment it looked as if he needed us.

Simon seated Jesus on the cushioned divan where he could rest his weary body next to Lazarus. The two embraced. Oh, that sight! I couldn't resist sitting down in front of them, listening in on their private exchanges and their joy at being together again. We laughed as Jesus mischievously offered Lazarus a yellow olive.

Remembering his jaundiced eyes, Lazarus cackled, "Never!"

We chuckled together about how the three of us never wanted to wear linen again. Jesus' fatigue and somberness seemed to lift, as if our few moments together were like a tonic of fresh, delicious wine.

Just then, some servant girls brought bowls of water to Jesus and the disciples with which to wash. Oh, no! I was so angry with myself! As usual, I had been more intent on being in the presence of my Lord than taking care of business. *What was wrong with me? Did I always have to lose track of time?* I looked toward the corner of the room. The basil springs Martha had picked were already wilting, and my alabaster jar still rested secretly beneath my cloak in the kitchen. It would have been the perfect time to carry out my plan.

Inwardly fuming, I started to get up to see to my task, but just then Martha directed the servers to parade out of the kitchen with the night's feast. I was furious with myself! My secret hope to anoint my brother, the guests, and my Lord was now dashed!

I ate my meal with a diminished appetite and tried to enjoy

the conversations around me without appearing to dampen the celebration. I was, nevertheless, preoccupied with my stupidity.

It was during the serving of the fruit and nuts that Simon stood up, asking for quiet among the guests.

It had not escaped anyone's notice that a large crowd had gathered outside his door, making noise and pushing against the entrance. Some even climbed up onto the roof to listen in on the conversations. Although he was a patient man, Simon's exasperation was becoming more evident as he tried to be heard in his own house.

"My family and my friends," he called out with a nervous but joy-filled voice, "I have welcomed you here tonight to celebrate my wondrous healing and the return from the dead of my friend, Lazarus, and to honor this man, Jesus, who made it all possible."

Several of us nodded our heads in exuberant agreement.

Simon continued: "For seven long years I wandered the Caves of the Unclean, excommunicated from all of you by the law of Moses, which says: 'The person with such an infectious disease must wear torn clothes, let his hair be unkempt, cover the lower part of his face and cry out, "Unclean, Unclean!" As long as he has the infection he remains unclean. He must live alone; he must live outside the camp.'"

Simon directed our attention to his family beside him. "For seven unbearable years, I was forced to leave behind my beloved Tirzah, my daughter Keturah, and our sons Nathan, and Samuel." His hurt rose in his eyes as the five of them remembered their shared agony.

"It was only several weeks ago that nine other men and I saw this man, Jesus, on a road with these disciples as he was entering a village on the border of Samaria. We had heard rumors of someone they called Messiah, healing the blind, raising the dead, and delivering many from demons. And so, without him knowing, the ten of us walked along behind him, watching miracle after miracle as people brought him the paralyzed, young children born blind, and old women who could no longer walk. We saw lame young girls dance with him after their healing, gray-haired grandfathers rise off their mats, and women healed instantaneously of torments in their minds.

"We started to believe because of these miracles. We cried out to him, calling to him from our required distance, pleading: 'Jesus, Master, have pity on us!'"

At this, Simon's head fell forward, and his chin began to quiver. He cleared his throat and attempted to say more, but the gesture of his hand moving to his heart said it all.

He finally continued: "It was when he turned toward us, and looked at us—looked at us in the eyes—that we began to believe in him. It wasn't because of the miracles, but because we saw...his heart."

I sat motionless, pondering the immensity of their suffering. For the first time in many years, someone had turned to look at them, not run from them. They'd been kicked, spat on, taunted, and beaten. They'd been insulted, hated, and ignored. To be noticed, to be heard, and to be acknowledged—it seemed that these gifts from Jesus were more important than the recovery of their physical bodies.

Simon continued: "We didn't dare approach him for fear that we would defile him," Simon related. "We were lepers. It had become *who* we were, not just *what* we were. And to be truthful, we were afraid. But very kindly, very simply, he just said, 'Go. Continue on your journey. Show yourselves to the priests.'

"It would be the priests' authoritative declaration of our healing that would allow us to get our lives back, but it was also a risk of further shunning should we still be declared unclean.

"We stopped walking to consult with each other. 'Should we trust this man?' we wondered. We didn't know him at all. We knew we would be pelted with trash, abused, and beaten even on our way to the priests. Would that be worth the cost?

"But, my friends," he said excitedly, "hope made us go—hope for a future, hope in a man, hope in a God that would someday answer our cries." Simon brushed more tears from his cheeks, which only served to make the pink of his face glow more vibrantly.

His eyes narrowed in remembrance, and his voice became softer. "On our way, as we obeyed what he had said to do, I felt my hands begin to itch. The fingers on my left hand had been gone for four years. Two were left on my right hand. Without looking I reached with my right hand to scratch the stump, and my fingers clasped together for the first time in years! My fingers . . . they had . . . just appeared! My hands were restored!"

He held his hand up and wiggled his fingers to demonstrate his claim. He laughed with a joy that infected everyone. The dinner guests were awed, and some started to clap.

"I stopped walking and started shouting! But that's not all!" Simon exclaimed as his voice became louder.

"My right ear had been disfigured, and I could no longer hear out of it, and my nose was almost completely gone. Immediately I had hearing in my ear. I reached up to touch my face and felt my nose, my beautiful, brown, protruding nose, completely re-created, and my ear had re-formed over the hole where I was deaf!"

Simon's family was now standing with him, wiping away their jubilant tears.

"When my friend, Manahem, turned to me to see why I was shouting, I saw his face made instantly whole and the disease vanish right before my eyes! I blinked, and he was changed! His left forearm that had been half-eaten away to the elbow was fully recovered!

"At the same time as our healing, Tobias ahead of us stumbled and fell down into the dirt because his new toes had gotten in the way of his walking crutch! His foot had returned, complete, whole, and without redness! All ten of us, from the youngest of 17 to the oldest of 67 were completely healed because this man . . . because this man turned toward us and loved us." Simon sucked in a quivering lungful of breath and broke down in tears.

The guests began to cheer, and some stood up, rushing to bow in front of the table. The revelation of who Jesus was went wafting through the air like a potent perfume, transfixing everyone. Before my eyes, I began to see them recognize that the fullness of the prophesies, the promised one throughout the ages in the Scripture, was sitting before them in a living room on a purple divan, nibbling on a green fig.

The power of hearing about miracle after miracle made my heart pound with faith. Simon, dead to all he cared about, stricken with a flesh-eating incurable disease, was now whole and hungry with an appetite to know and honor the one who had loved him back to life. Lazarus, my dearest brother, carrying within his body the death-sentence of our father, his body decaying just as Simon's, was called to walk out of the tomb back into light and life. Both men had been dying or dead, both now were alive and worshipping the true Messiah, Lord of the living and the dead!

He had truly "turned our mourning into dancing," as the prophet Jeremiah had foretold!

But would that promise hold true and yield a miracle for Jesus himself?

Brandied pears were being served and the music had again begun when I looked over at Jesus and caught his eye. A deep seriousness filled his face that didn't seem to come from the toll of his celebrity nor the fatigue of his travels. Through a silent exchange of his eyes with mine, he let me know that he, too, was soon headed toward a tomb. Everyone else was celebrating life while this solitary life-giver was preparing to lay his down. The thought cut me deep inside my being.

For months, whenever he would speak, the disciples, Lazarus, Martha, and I had felt as if he had been speaking in code, in language containing hidden messages. But lately he had spoken plainly: "We are going to Jerusalem, and the Son of Man will be betrayed to the chief priests and the teachers of the law. They will condemn him to death and will turn him over to the Gentiles to be mocked and flogged and crucified. On the third day he will be raised to life!" That night my heart understood that it would soon come to pass.

There was such presence in the room right then that I felt as if my mind and heart were in tune with a momentum beyond my control. Something holy was happening, despite my protestations. Everything in me wanted to rush to him, to comfort him and maybe even dissuade him. The feverish intuition I had about his impending death felt identical to my former gnawing concern over Lazarus' illness.

After my brother's resurrection, I saw that something bigger was taking place than what we understood. A larger picture began to emerge than what I had formerly comprehended. It dawned on me that Lazarus might be a forerunner of Jesus, and if that were so, then this man's body would have to be broken and poured out in order to fulfill his unique destiny.

Almost as if it were a cue, I had an impulse to leave the room. As I stood up, the eyes of my Master seemed to steady me, for I was internally quaking.

I hurried to the kitchen and quickly threw aside the wraps hiding my alabaster jar. As I bent down to reach for it, the fabric ribbon in my hair loosened, and my hair fell across my shoulders. I quickly tied it back again, happy that no one had seen me. It was quite scandalous to allow one's hair to flow freely in our culture. It was a sign of a lurid life, someone with a sensuous past. God knew I was not one of those women, for I had saved my heart for one who never came. But as I stood there, reaching for my inheritance, I knew there was one who had truly captured my heart, not for this world, but for the world to come. I was finally ready to show him the extent of my love.

Martha had walked past me into the kitchen to prepare the heated wine. I could tell her inclination was to chide me for not sprinkling the perfume on the guests, but she instead smiled and nodded her head, as if I were competent to decide what to do.

The flickering light from the oil lamps in the house made the alabaster appear to glow in the dark. I held it out from myself, looking at its porcelain-like luminescence. The two thin handles on either side of the container each formed what looked like half a heart. A long, stately neck emerged out of the top with a sealed opening from which the golden nard would flow. I held it to my chest one last time, rejoicing that this small token of love would be given to one who had given life to me.

My joy began to escalate as I reached to peel off the seal, but my hands were trembling too much to be able to uncork the top. I found a knife in the kitchen, but the container had been sealed for so long I didn't know how to release the flow. The cork and wax had become almost one and had completely plugged up the neck of the vase! My heart began to pound, and I was frustrated with how hard it was to expose my deepest treasure.

"Open up, now!" I commanded beneath my breath.

The Anointing

It was no use. I had no time to dig out the layers of waxed cork. There had to be another way. I nervously looked toward the banquet room and saw that some were beginning to stir, preparing to leave. Was Jesus about to stand up? I had to go to him!

I took a deep breath, picked up my vial, walked into the crowded room, and headed for the Master.

Judas Iscariot was sitting very near the Lord, and when I entered, he broke off his conversation and watched me with suspicion as I drew nearer to Jesus.

The chattering in the room stopped, Martha told me later, but I didn't notice. The only thing that mattered was giving my Lord my greatest gift—my heart, my inheritance, my every point of worth. I was giving him all I had. I was giving him myself.

As I came up behind Jesus, he didn't seem to notice. I wanted to reach out to touch his hair and comfort his head, but instead I reached for my alabaster, and with all the strength in my grip, I broke the neck of the jar I had waited all my life to enjoy.

Immediately, there arose a scent of such strength that everyone nearby, including Jesus, inhaled deeply. The air was humid with the scent of patchouli, cloves, musk, and aloe wood—the most precious mixture of ointment that could be enjoyed. Before he could even turn around to look, I poured the container upside down over my Lord's head.

It was as if all time stopped. The flow of the perfume was thinner than honey, but thicker than milk. I watched the amber glow of the liquid take its time trailing down that precious chiseled face, through his dirty beard, into the crease of his neck, and down his chest. Because the bottle had been irregularly broken, the oil was flowing over my own hands and down my elbows as well, then onto his back, and the linen sash around his waist.

The fragrance was overpowering, and the eyes of who were nearby began to water from the potency of its scent.

Mine were watering with real tears.

As I looked more closely at Jesus, so were his.

I was delirious with a paradoxical joy and grief, as if every ounce that poured out was both a gift of love as well as a symbol of imminent death.

I stopped pouring and stood shaking for a moment, feeling almost intoxicated, before I walked around to the front edge of his seat. The astonished guests moved out of my way.

I knelt down and removed his torn, dusty sandals. I held the broken bottle to my chest one last time, then with all the pleasure I had ever known, spilled the remaining contents of the alabaster onto those most precious feet.

Down over his ankles, off the edge of his heel and toes, the ointment dripped like amber-colored blood.

Even with my entire offering—with giving him my most priceless treasure—it still didn't feel like any of this came close to expressing my deep gratitude for bringing back my brother, and my joy in knowing this man as my Lord and Messiah.

It was when I had finished pouring that I looked up to see his full face. His eyes were closed. He was experiencing every drop and each sensation to its fullest—absorbing, submitting, and receiving the depth of my worship into himself.

It then became clear to me that this act of devotion would not be complete without my sacrificing the one point of self-worship I still had clung to in my life—my hair. My family knew that I considered my hair to be my glory. It had been my favorite thing about myself. I always made sure it was scented and properly arranged. But in that indescribable moment, something called out and made me even want to give him more—give him my social decorum, give him my reputation, give him my vanity.

I heard a few gasps and some murmuring as I gently untied my long dark tresses and shook my head, letting them fall over my face and onto his golden feet.

This had been our place, our mutual point of contact—not his lips, not his head, not his hands—but his feet. My unbridled hair fell to create an inner chamber for my lips and his feet. My love for him was finally unrestrained. A new melody began deep within my breast, and my head began to sway back and forth to its rhythm. I closed my eyes, lost in this bridal chamber. I couldn't stop kissing his toes, his feet, and his ankles. My face rested on the top of his left foot. I gently turned it over so my cheek could fit more easily into the arch. Silent tears fell from my eyes.

With each movement of my head up and down his feet, I felt as if the hard waxed seal that had stopped up my heart was being pried open and uncorked. For the first time, I was able to pour out my adoring love and worship and have it be received by the one who created me to be completely me. Worshipping him that way in that moment was worth every ounce of precious perfume and every measure of earthly inheritance.

In contrast to my most exquisite joy just seconds before, deep sobs arose within me when I saw the small bleeding laceration on the top of his right foot. I began to remember the words he had said: "The Son of Man will be crucified." I wept, writhing internally, praying, pleading, and begging God to save him. In my heart I knew it was futile. The momentum of the bigger story was escalating with every moment.

My tears splashed into the nard, but it was like oil mixing with vinegar. I wept for the pain he was going to endure. I wept for the people who would do the deed. And I wept for us who would lose the Savior who miraculously healed lepers and the friend who laughed out loud while offering a yellow olive.

I kissed the small cut one last time and patted the blood dry with my hair. Massaging the rest of his foot with my hands, I rubbed deep into his skin the extract that would linger with him even through his death on the cross.

I had sacrificed my very best for him. I knew intuitively he would soon sacrifice his very best for me.

As I lifted my head, my hair felt heavy, saturated with the weight of the oil. Unbeknownst to me, the oil had cascaded down my own face and neck and across my arms. The aroma had stopped burning my eyes, but I had to keep blinking to be able to see him.

Jesus was completely still and looked as if he weren't breathing. I closed my eyes again. My head and heart were swirling, as if I were dancing with a presence that had no form but enfolded me with every breath. I wanted to linger there, like the perfume in the air, and absorb this moment forever. But a rude voice interrupted our spirit-to-spirit dance.

"Why this waste of perfume?" demanded Judas Iscariot.

"It could have been sold for a year's wages and given to the poor!" someone across the room yelled indignantly. Instantaneous anger shot throughout the room, especially from the disciples, which surprised and wounded me.

Jesus rose with lightening speed to his feet. "Leave her alone!" he commanded. "She has done a beautiful thing for me. The poor you will always have with you, but you will not always have me!"

He looked directly into my eyes and lowered his voice as if to quiet me. "When she poured this perfume on my body, she did it to prepare me for my burial."

He stared back at his disciples, who looked mystified. "I tell you the truth, wherever this gospel is preached throughout the world, what she has done will also be told in memory of her."

As the disciples backed down, my heart rose up.

Jesus took my hands to lift me to my feet. Both of us had to hold tight because the oil made our hands slippery. I clung with all my might to him, and he lifted me out of condemnation and brought me back into a position of honor and approval, simply because I loved him.

I decided, from that day on, to let my curls run free, free to let them be how they were created to be.

And so did Martha.

It took many months before the scent of nard was no longer noticeable in my hair.

What I hadn't counted on that day was that his anointing had ended up becoming my anointing.

I died to having my own agenda, to religious expectations, and I died to my pride that day. However, I didn't die to die. I died to live!

His fragrance, like the perfume, stayed with me until the day of Pentecost, when his presence descended again, this time like a rushing wind, and filled me afresh with the perfume and power of his irresistible, unconditional love.

I still have the broken alabaster. It was later that night after the "anointing" that I looked inside the neck of the bottle.

The waxed cork had mysteriously disappeared.

Perhaps Jesus heals in more ways than one.

REFLECTIONS

"The Anointing"

1. Mary's treasure was in her alabaster jar. Where does your heart go for comfort, pleasure, worth or meaning?

    Your talent?
    Intelligence?
    Reputation?
    Ministry?
    Children?
    Career?
    Looks?
    Finances?
    Friendships?
    Relationship?

2. Like Mary, are there things you've heard from the Lord that you resist embracing?

3. Can you relate to Lazarus, having experienced a healing or gift of some kind and being put on the spot to share about it? Are you more like Simon who returned to thank the Lord or like the other nine who didn't?

4. Like Simon, have you called yourself "unclean?" (Have others?)

5. Has your uncleanness of body or heart eaten away your worthiness to be loved (or even noticed)? He sees you. Just as he did with Simon, he's waiting to make you whole, too!

6. Like Mary's alabaster, has the container of your heart been sealed off so long you don't know how to release the flow of your love?

7. Are you willing to risk ignoring social decorum in order to lavish your love on others?

8. In your obedience to love God and others, are you willing to experience being reviled, even by those who are close to Christ?

9. What point of self-worship do you hold onto the most?

10. Are you willing to release it to fully worship him?

Hair, in the scripture, is symbolic of thought. Would you like his presence to soak your thoughts? Do you want your mind to be intoxicated with the fragrance of his character and the potency of his affection? Right now, ask the Holy Spirit to pour his oil over your head. Allow his fragrant love to seep into your tired thinking, your damaged emotions, your aching and wounded body. Feel the treasure of his healing balm trickle down over you and ask the Lord to open your heart to receive all he has to give you.

He was anointed for burial so that you may life life in his resurrection power. Ask him to enlarge your capacity to receive all he has to pour out on you!

Epilogue

Although there's no further mention of me in the sacred writings, the legacy of Jesus healing my "issue" lives on. Women and men across the world and throughout time have also encountered this Jesus and have had their "issue" instantaneously or progressively transformed.

As I watch from my point of view in heaven, along with a mass of spectators who are cheering you on, I'm standing up straight and tall with the voice of personal experience to declare:

Jesus, the Messiah, reigns in heaven and on earth. His kingdom *will* come and his purpose *will* be done in *your* personal earth—your body, mind, emotions, and spirit—just as it was in my earthly frame and is now manifested in my heavenly one!

He is not unmindful of your pain anymore than he was of mine. Look up. His astonishing eyes are on you right now. Press in and reach for him in prayer. Tell him the truth of your need. You can see, from my story, he specializes in encounters of the heart. And just like me, you'll find there's more to *your* story than meets the eye!

—*The Woman Without an Issue*

Endnotes

[1] *A Commentary on the New Testament from the Talmud and Hebraica, Exercitations upon the Gospel of St. Mark,* Chapters 5-8, John Lightfoot, Philologos Religious Online Books, Philologos.org.

[2] "Mary the Heroine of Bethany and Her Immortal Deed, Lesson 85," Dr. Albert Long, written to the *S.S. Times* from Constantinople. See "The Life of Christ in the Synoptic Gospels," www.studyjesus.com

About the Author

CATHY HEILIGER is a popular speaker, and the director of women's ministry at the Inland Vineyard Christian Fellowship in Corona, California. She has had a 25-year ministry in emotional healing, is a certified professional life-coach, and has been trained in the craft of screenwriting. Cathy and her husband, Bruce, have two married children and three granddaughters.

Contact the author at:
www.cathyheiliger.com